Master Your Maths

Mental maths and problem-solving activities

Eamonn Brennan • Meriel McCord
Deirdre Mulligan • Andrée Mulvihill

CJ Fallon
ESTABLISHED 1895

Published by

CJ Fallon
Ground Floor – Block B
Liffey Valley Office Campus
Dublin 22

ISBN: 978-0-7144-2170-4

First Edition March 2016
This Reprint April 2021

Introduction

Master Your Maths is a series of workbooks providing the most effective and structured daily mental maths and problem-solving programme. Each book is based on 30 weeks of the school year, comprising mental maths and problem-solving exercises for Monday to Thursday, along with a Friday test. The questions are varied and increase in complexity as the year progresses. **Master Your Maths** provides daily questions where children can develop problem-solving skills. It helps teachers create a classroom culture where children are encouraged to develop as independent mathematicians with strong problem-solving skills.

Master Your Maths:

- covers all strands and strand units of the maths curriculum.
- develops and reinforces mental calculation, concepts and skills.
- provides daily practice in problem-solving which is the key to maths understanding and higher scores in maths.
- provides real-life problems where children can see the role of maths in everyday life.
- provides Friday test pages to assess learning.
- provides assessment record sheets where children can track their own progress.

Contents

Individual Pupil Record

Week 1		Week 2		Week 3		Week 4		Week 5	
Date:		Date:		Date:		Date:		Date:	
Mon	12	Mon	12	Mon	12	Mon	12	Mon	12
Tues	12	Tues	12	Tues	12	Tues	12	Tues	12
Wed	12	Wed	12	Wed	12	Wed	12	Wed	12
Thurs	12	Thurs	12	Thurs	12	Thurs	12	Thurs	12
Fri	15	Fri	15	Fri	15	Fri	15	Fri	15

Week 6		Week 7		Week 8		Week 9		Week 10	
Date:		Date:		Date:		Date:		Date:	
Mon	12	Mon	12	Mon	12	Mon	12	Mon	12
Tues	12	Tues	12	Tues	12	Tues	12	Tues	12
Wed	12	Wed	12	Wed	12	Wed	12	Wed	12
Thurs	12	Thurs	12	Thurs	12	Thurs	12	Thurs	12
Fri	15	Fri	15	Fri	15	Fri	15	Fri	15

Week 11		Week 12		Week 13		Week 14		Week 15	
Date:		Date:		Date:		Date:		Date:	
Mon	12	Mon	12	Mon	12	Mon	12	Mon	12
Tues	12	Tues	12	Tues	12	Tues	12	Tues	12
Wed	12	Wed	12	Wed	12	Wed	12	Wed	12
Thurs	12	Thurs	12	Thurs	12	Thurs	12	Thurs	12
Fri	15	Fri	15	Fri	15	Fri	15	Fri	15

Week 16		Week 17		Week 18		Week 19		Week 20	
Date:		**Date:**		**Date:**		**Date:**		**Date:**	
Mon	12	Mon	12	Mon	12	Mon	12	Mon	12
Tues	12	Tues	12	Tues	12	Tues	12	Tues	12
Wed	12	Wed	12	Wed	12	Wed	12	Wed	12
Thurs	12	Thurs	12	Thurs	12	Thurs	12	Thurs	12
Fri	15	Fri	15	Fri	15	Fri	15	Fri	15

Week 21		Week 22		Week 23		Week 24		Week 25	
Date:		**Date:**		**Date:**		**Date:**		**Date:**	
Mon	12	Mon	12	Mon	12	Mon	12	Mon	12
Tues	12	Tues	12	Tues	12	Tues	12	Tues	12
Wed	12	Wed	12	Wed	12	Wed	12	Wed	12
Thurs	12	Thurs	12	Thurs	12	Thurs	12	Thurs	12
Fri	15	Fri	15	Fri	15	Fri	15	Fri	15

Week 26		Week 27		Week 28		Week 29		Week 30	
Date:		**Date:**		**Date:**		**Date:**		**Date:**	
Mon	12	Mon	12	Mon	12	Mon	12	Mon	12
Tues	12	Tues	12	Tues	12	Tues	12	Tues	12
Wed	12	Wed	12	Wed	12	Wed	12	Wed	12
Thurs	12	Thurs	12	Thurs	12	Thurs	12	Thurs	12
Fri	15	Fri	15	Fri	15	Fri	15	Fri	15

Monday

1. It is ___ o'clock.

2. 2 + 5 = ___

3. 3 + 3 = ___

4. Colour the rectangle red.

5. 9 – 2 = ___

6. Colour the even number.

⑪ ⑬ ⑫ ⑰ ⑨

7. Write the numeral twenty-two.

___

8. What number comes next?

2, 4, 6, 8, ___

9. Tick the heavier object.

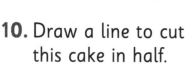 □   □

10. Draw a line to cut this cake in half.

11. Laura has six apples. Kelly has two apples. How many apples have they altogether? ___

12. There were seven birds on a branch. Two birds flew away. How many were left? ___

/12

Tuesday

1. Draw hands on the clock to show 2 o'clock.

2. 4 + 4 = ___

3. 8 add 1 = ___

4. Colour the square blue.

5. 13 – 6 = ___

6. Colour the odd number.

⑯ ⑱ ⑥ ⑦ ⑧

7. Join the dots.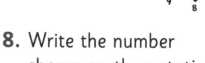

8. Write the number shown on the notation board. ___

t	u
	●
	●
	●
●	●
●	●

9. What number comes next? 1, 3, 5, 7, ___

10. Tick the lighter animal.

 □   □

Jack had three apples. Mary had six apples.

11. How many apples had Jack and Mary altogether? ___

12. How many more apples does Mary have than Jack? ___

/12

Wednesday

1. Show 45 on the notation board.

t	u

2. 2 + 3 = ____

3. It is ____ o'clock.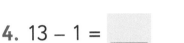

4. 13 − 1 = ____

5. Count the money.

____

6. Colour the 4th car yellow.

7. 2 + 2 + 2 = ____

8. Colour the triangle green.

9. Tick the container that holds more.

10. Write the missing numbers.

23, 24, 25, ____ , ____ , 28

11. James has 4 crayons. Seán has 4 more than that. How many crayons has Seán? ____

12. Helen has 5c. A rubber costs 7c. How much more does Helen need to buy the rubber? ____

/12

Thursday

1. Write the number shown on the abacus. ____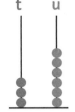

2. 2 + 7 = ____

3. 9 take away 3 = ____

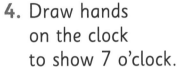

4. Draw hands on the clock to show 7 o'clock.

5. Colour the rectangle red.

6. Tick the container that holds less.

7. Draw the other half of this picture.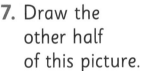

8. 14 − 5 = ____

9. 2 + 2 + 2 + 2 = ____

10. Colour the coins to make 14c.

There are 8 dogs, 3 cats and 1 goldfish in a pet shop.

11. How many animals altogether are in the pet shop? ____

12. How many fewer cats than dogs are in the pet shop? ____

/12

Monday

1. 4 + 3 = ____

2. 9 – 4 = ____

3. What time is it? ____ o'clock

4. Circle the odd number.

   5   8   10

5. Write the numeral twenty. ____

6. Colour the semi-circle green.

   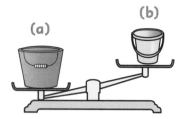

7. 0, 3, 6, ____, 12

8. Which is the 1st month of the year?
   ☐ January ☐ February ☐ May

9. 6 + 6 = ____

10. Which bucket is heavier? ____

    (b)
    (a)

11. Jamie had 10c. He bought an apple for 5c. How much change did he get? ____

12. Jason has 3 cards, Jack has 5 cards and Ellen has 7 cards. How many cards have they altogether? ____

/12

8

Tuesday

1. Add 4 to 5. ____

2. 8 – 3 = ____

3. Draw a triangle.

4. 4, 7, 10, ____, 16

5. Join the dots.

   20·   21· ·11   ·12
   19·   ·13
   18·   17· 15· ·14
        ·16
                ·10

6. Count the money. ____

7. What time is it? ____ o'clock

8. Circle the even number.

   3   9   12

9. Write the number shown on the notation board. ____

   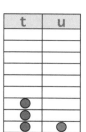

10. 7 + 7 = ____

Patrick has 5c. John has 7c. Lisa has 3c.

11. How much money have they altogether? ____

12. If they decided to buy a skipping rope that cost 20c, how much more money would they need? ____

/12

Wednesday

1. 6 + 3 = ____

2. 10 − 3 = ____

3. What time is it?
   ____ o'clock

4. Circle the odd number.

   18   11   20

5. Show 28 on the abacus.

6. 8 + 8 = ____

7. How many corners has a rectangle? ____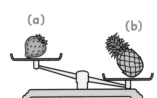

8. 3 + 3 + 3 = ____

9. Circle every 3rd number.

   1 2 3 4 5 6 7 8 9

10. Which fruit is lighter? ____ (a) (b)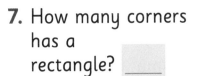

11. Jim has 10 marbles. Jane has 4 marbles. How many more marbles has Jim than Jane? ____

12. Emma started at the number 8. She jumped forward 2 steps and then back 1 step. What number did she end up at? ____

   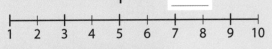
   1 2 3 4 5 6 7 8 9 10

/12

Thursday

1. Add 4 to 7. ____

2. 9 + 9 = ____

3. What time is it?
   ____ o'clock

4. Circle the even number.

   24   21   23

5. Write 18 in words.
   _____

6. How many sides has a square? ____

7. 4 + 4 + 4 = ____

8. Which month comes after February?

   ☐ January

   ☐ March

   ☐ April

9. Take 4 from 8. ____

10. Tick the longer line.

   ☐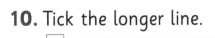

   ☐

THE SHOP

Lollipop 5c   **Ice-cream** 10c

Popcorn 6c   **Water** 15c

11. How much for a lollipop and a popcorn? ____

12. How much for water and an ice-cream? ____

/12

See page 67 for test.

Monday

1. It is _____ past _____.

2. 5 + 6 = _____

3. 9 take away 3 = _____

☆ ☆ ☆ ✦ ✦ ✦ ✦ ✦

4. 3 **tens** 8 **units** = _____

5. Colour the 2c coins to make 8c.

6. _____ + _____ = 6
   so $\frac{1}{2}$ of 6 is _____.

7. 5, 10, 15, _____, _____

8. Colour the longer scarf red.
   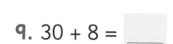
   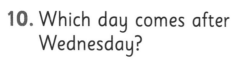

9. 30 + 8 = _____

10. Which day comes after Wednesday?
    ☐ Friday   ☐ Thursday

11. There are 5 spots on a ladybird. How many spots are there on three ladybirds? _____

12. 10 pencils fit in a box. I have 3 pencils. How many more do I need to fill the box? _____

/12

Tuesday

1. Draw hands on the clock to show $\frac{1}{2}$ past 7.

2. 6 + 6 = _____

3. 10 – 4 = _____

4. 5 **tens** 3 **units** = _____

5. How much do the apple and the pear cost altogether? _____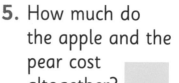

6. 6 + _____ = 12
   so $\frac{1}{2}$ of 12 is _____.

7. Circle the animal that is heavier.
   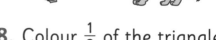

8. Colour $\frac{1}{2}$ of the triangle.

9. 12, 14, 16, _____, _____

10. Which day comes before Saturday?
    ☐ Sunday   ☐ Friday

Pets

dog	🐕	🐕	🐕	🐕
cat	🐈	🐈		
bird	🐦	🐦	🐦	

11. How many children have a dog or a cat? _____

12. How many children have a bird or a dog? _____

/12

Wednesday

1. It is _____ past _____.

2. Write the number shown on the abacus. _____

3. Add 6 and 5. _____

4. $12 - 7 =$ _____

5. How much? _____

6. Colour the 2nd penguin.

7. 12 count on $10 =$ _____

8. Colour the animal that is lighter.

9. Colour $\frac{1}{2}$ of the stars.

10. Which day comes between Tuesday and Thursday?

☐ Friday ☐ Monday
☐ Wednesday

11. Louise bought 3 buns costing 10c each. How much did they cost altogether? _____

12. Hasan had 7 grapes. He gave 3 grapes to Melanie. How many has he left? _____

/12

Thursday

1. Draw hands on the clock to show $\frac{1}{2}$ past 9.

2. $19 - 6 =$ _____

3. 13 take away $4 =$ _____

4. Show 56 on the abacus.

5. Colour the 5c coins to make 15c.

6. 16, 18, 20, _____, _____

7. $50 + 4 =$ _____

8. Colour $\frac{1}{2}$ of the teddy bears.

9. $12 +$ _____ $= 15$

10.
```
 t u
 2 4
+1 2
_____
```

11. How much do a carton of apple juice and a carton of orange juice cost altogether? _____

12. Molly has 50c. How much change will she get if she buys the carton of apple juice and the carton of orange juice? _____

/12

See page 68 for test.

Monday

1. What time is it? ____ past ____

2. 7 + 6 = ____

3. 14 − 6 = ____

4. 2 **tens** 5 **units** = ____

5. Colour the 10c coins to make 30c.

6. Colour $\frac{1}{2}$ of the square.

7. How many edges has a cuboid? ____

8. Colour the 4th dog.

9. 30 + 4 = ____

10. Which is the 3rd month of the year?

☐ March ☐ February
☐ September

11. If you have 10 bananas and you want to share them among 5 children, how many does each child get? ____

12. John has 12 stickers. How many more does he need to make 20?

____

/12

Tuesday

1. Draw hands on the clock to show $\frac{1}{2}$ past 7.

2. Add 9 and 8. ____

3. Which is the 2nd month of the year?
☐ January ☐ July ☐ February

4. 10 subtract 2. ____

5. How many? ____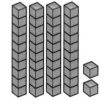

6. How much? ____

7. Colour $\frac{1}{2}$ of this set of balls.

8. How many faces has a cube? ____

9. Which is heavier? ____

(a)   (b)

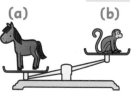

10. 40 + 5 = ____

APRIL						
Mon	Tue	Wed	Thurs	Fri	Sat	Sun
		1	2	3	4	5	6
7	8	9	10	11	12	13
14	15	16	17	18	19	20
21	22	23	24	25	26	27
28	29	30				

11. On what day does the 12th of April fall? ____

12. What date is the first Saturday in April? ____

/12

Wednesday

1. What time is it?

   _____ past _____

2. $16 - 9 =$ _____

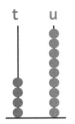

3. Write the number shown on the abacus. _____

4. Colour the coins to make 45c.

5. Colour half the semi-circle.

6. $4 + 7 =$ _____

7. Colour the sphere.

8. Circle the odd number.

   28   10   12   21

9. Write these numbers in order, starting with the smallest: 35, 53, 47. _____ , _____ , _____

10. $19 - 12 =$ _____

11. Lucy bought an apple for 30c and a banana for 35c. How much change did she get back from 70c? _____

12. A farmer put 3 horses, 2 cows and 1 goat in a shed. How many legs have they altogether? _____

/12

Thursday

1. Draw hands on the clock to show $\frac{1}{2}$ past 4.

2. Add 6 and 8. _____

3. Which is the 5th month of the year?

   ☐ May   ☐ June   ☐ March

4. Subtract 8 from 16. _____

5. How many? _____

6. How much? _____

7. Colour $\frac{1}{2}$ of the circle.

8. Name the shape. _____

9. Which is lighter? _____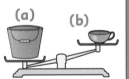

   (a)   (b)

10. $20 + 7 =$ _____

At the circus, a clown blew up 14 green balloons, 15 red balloons and 11 blue balloons.

11. How many balloons did he blow up altogether? _____

12. How many more red balloons than blue balloons did he blow up? _____

/12

See page 69 for test.

Monday

1. How much? _____

2. Fill in the missing sign (<, >, =).
   5 _____ 7

3. $13 - \underline{} = 4$

4. $34 = \underline{}$ tens _____ units

5. Colour the cube.

6. Write these numbers in order, starting with the largest:
   34, 16, 25, 36, 4.
   _____ , _____ , _____ , _____ , _____

7. Colour $\frac{1}{2}$ of the set.

8. $6 + 5 + 4 = \underline{}$

9. Which holds more water? _____

   (a)    (b)

10. t u
    2 5
    +1 3
    _____

11. What must I add to 12 to make 18? _____

12. Maria had 12 strawberries. She gave half of them to her brother. How many has she left? _____

/12

Tuesday

1. 10, 15, 20, _____ , _____

2. $4 + 8 + 6 = \boxed{}$

3. Write the numeral thirty-two. _____

4. Draw hands on the clock to show $\frac{1}{2}$ an hour later than 3 o'clock.

5. $14 - 8 = \underline{}$

6. Colour $\frac{1}{2}$ of the set.

7. 7 add 5 = _____

8. Colour the cuboid.

9. Circle the shortest snake.

10. 3 tens 8 units = _____

Favourite fruit

apples	🍎	🍎	🍎	🍎	🍎	🍎	
oranges	🍊	🍊	🍊				
bananas	🍌	🍌	🍌	🍌	🍌	🍌	🍌

11. How many children prefer apples and bananas? _____

12. How many fewer children prefer oranges than bananas? _____

/12

Wednesday

1. 15, 20, 25, _____, _____

2. 3 + 8 = _____

3. Which is lighter, your schoolbag or your pencil? _____

4. How much? _____

5. Colour $\frac{1}{2}$ of the set.

6. Write the number that comes after twenty-six. _____

7. Draw hands on the clock to show $\frac{1}{2}$ an hour earlier than $\frac{1}{2}$ past 5.

8.
```
 t u
 4 5
+3 4
─────
```

9. Round 25 to the nearest 10. _____

10. Fill in the missing sign (<, >, =).
    16 _____ 11 + 4

11. There were 8 slices of pizza. Daddy ate half of them. How many were left? _____

12. Mary has:
    Matthew has:
    How much do they have altogether? _____

/12

Thursday

1. 7 + 7 = _____

2. 15 take away 5 = _____

3. 20, 25, 30, _____, _____

4. Draw hands on the clock to show $\frac{1}{2}$ an hour later than $\frac{1}{2}$ past 4.

5. Show 46 on the abacus.

t   u

6. Colour the sphere.

7. Write these numbers in order, starting with the largest: 35, 53, 43, 26, 12.
   _____, _____, _____, _____, _____

8.
```
 t u
 4 6
+2 3
─────
```

9. Write the numbers between 48 and 55. _____

10. Colour $\frac{1}{2}$ of the set.

11. Ellen cooked 32 vegetable pies. She sold 17 of them. How many has she left? _____

12. There were 16 birds on a wire. 8 more arrived and 4 flew away. How many were left on the wire? _____

/12

See page 70 for test.

Monday

1. How many 2c coins make up 10c? **5**

2. 10, 20, 30, **40**, 50

3. Add 17 and 8. **25**

4. Take away 9 from 21. **12**

5. Write these numbers in order, starting with the largest:
17, 23, 14, 12, 27.
27 , **23** , **17** , **14** , **12**

6. Colour $\frac{1}{2}$ of the set.

7. What time is it?
$\frac{1}{2}$ past **6**

8. Write the number that comes just before 48. **47**

9. Colour the cylinder.

10. Fill in the missing sign (<, >, =).
25 – 3 **=** 11 + 11

11. James read 18 books. Laura read 19 books and Jason read 23 books. How many books did they read altogether? **50**

12. Mary had 35 stickers. Joan had 11 fewer. How many had Joan?
24

/12

Tuesday

1. 2c + 2c + 1c + **5** = 10c

2. Subtract 7 from 19. **12**

3. Write these numbers in order, starting with the smallest:
23, 28, 24, 21, 30.
21 , **23** , **24** , **28** , **30**

4. Write the number that comes just after 18. **19**

5. Which shape can roll?

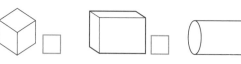

6. 25, 35, 45, **55** , 65

7. Add 16 and 9. **25**

8. Colour $\frac{1}{2}$ of the set.

9. Draw hands on the clock to show $\frac{1}{2}$ past 9.

10. Round 16 to the nearest 10. **20**

Andrew has 19 marbles. Sophie has 16 marbles. David has 21 marbles.

11. How many marbles have they altogether? **56**

12. If Sophie got 7 more marbles, how many would she have then?
23

/12

Wednesday

1. How many 5c coins make up 20c? **4**

2. 2, 12, 22, 32, **42**

3. Add 21 and 8. **29**

4. Subtract 9 from 22. **13**

5. Write these numbers in order, starting with the smallest: 37, 22, 30, 25, 31.

   22 , **25** , **31** , **37** , **30**

6. Colour $\frac{1}{2}$ of the set.

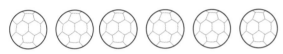

7. What time is it?

   _____ past _____

8. Write the number that comes just before 32. _____

9. Colour the shape that has no corners.

10. Your principal weighs:
    ☐ less than 1kg.
    ☐ more than 1kg.
    ☐ about 1kg.

11. Pete read 22 books. Liam read 14 books. How many books did they read altogether? _____

12. Emily is 9 years old. Her brother is 4 years older than her. How old is her brother? _____

/12

Thursday

1. Colour the 5c coins to make 20c.

2. Colour $\frac{1}{2}$ of the set.

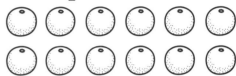

3. Draw hands on the clock to show half an hour earlier than half past 8.

4. Write the number that comes just after 25. _____

5. Colour the cube.

6. Add 15 and 8. _____

7. Fill in the missing sign (<, >, =).
   12 + 3 _____ 3 + 11

8. 20, 30, 40, 50, _____

9. Subtract 11 from 25. _____

10. Write these numbers in order, starting with the largest: 41, 53, 39, 52, 47.

    _____ , _____ , _____ , _____ , _____

Ann bought 9 flowers at 2c each.

11. How much did Ann spend? _____

12. How much change did she get back from 50c? _____

/12

Monday

1. Fill in the missing number from this section of the hundred square.

22	23	24
32	33	34
42		44

2. Which is the odd number: 30, 31 or 36? ____

3. 67 + 3 = ____

4. What time is it? ____ o'clock

5. 54 − 10 = ____

6. When I put two semi-circles together, I get a ____.

7. t u
  3 8
−1 6
____

8. There are ____ seasons in a year.

9. Fill in the missing sign (<, >, =).
8 + 2 ____ 12 − 4

10. When I add two odd numbers, the answer is always ____ (odd/even).

11. Mammy shared 16c equally between Sarah and Michelle. How much did each get? ____

12. A copy costs 20c. How many copies can I buy with 45c? ____

/12

Tuesday

1. Draw the other half of this shape.

2. Which is the even number: 51, 52 or 53? ____

3. 42 + 8 = ____

4. When I add two even numbers, the answer is always ____ (odd/even).

5. 72 − 10 = ____

6. A 2-D shape with 3 straight sides is a ____.

7. 23 + 5 = ____

8. Which is the last month of the year?
☐ January
☐ December
☐ November

9. Fill in the missing sign (<, >, =).
4 + 5 ____ 9 − 2

10. 7 **tens** 8 **units** = ____

Favourite activities

Football	⚽	⚽	⚽	⚽	⚽	⚽	⚽	⚽
Tennis	⊘	⊘	⊘	⊘	⊘			
Hurling	✓	✓	✓	✓				
Swimming	🏊	🏊	🏊	🏊	🏊	🏊	🏊	

11. How many children prefer football and tennis? ____

12. How many more children prefer swimming than hurling? ____

/12

Wednesday

1. Colour the shape that can't stack.

2. Which is the odd number: 41, 48 or 46? _____

3. Fill in the missing numbers from this section of the hundred square.

	62	63	64
71			

4. 97 + 3 = _____

5. 19 − 10 = _____

6. A circle has _____ corners.

7. 27 + 8 = _____

8. July is in the season of _____.

9. Fill in the missing sign (<, >, =).
   12 + 3 _____ 10 + 5

10. Draw hands on the clock to show $\frac{1}{2}$ an hour later than 7 o'clock.

11. Jim has 28 cards. Sam has 20 more than Jim. How many cards has Sam? _____

12. If one bar of chocolate costs 10c, how much would 7 bars cost? _____

/12

Thursday

1. Draw the other half of this picture.

2. Which is the even number: 10, 11 or 13? _____

3. Fill in the missing numbers from this section of the hundred square.

	45	46	
54			57
		66	

4. 76 + 4 = _____

5. 48 − 10 = _____

6. A rectangle has _____ sides.

7. 49 − 7 = _____

8. There are _____ months in a year.

9. Fill in the missing sign (<, >, =).
   15 − 5 _____ 13 + 5

10. Draw hands on the clock to show $\frac{1}{2}$ past 11.

Jackie has 20c, Michael has 15c and Lisa has 25c.

11. How much money have they altogether? _____

12. If a ball costs 75c, how much more would they need to buy it? _____

/12

See page 72 for test.

Monday

1. 5, 10, 15, 20, _____

2. 6 **tens** 9 **units** = _____

3. Draw a line of symmetry.

4. t u
    6 8
    −4 4
    _____

5. Finish this pattern.

     _____

6. Draw hands on the clock to show 6 o'clock.

7. Colour half the rectangle.

8. 35c = ◯ + ◯ + ◯

9. Fill in this section of the hundred square.

12		14	15
		24	25

10. 9 + 7 + 3 = _____

11. There were 65 people on a bus. 24 of them got off. How many were on the bus then? _____

12. Tara had 42 stamps. She got 28 stamps from Ian. How many stamps had she then? _____

/12

Tuesday

1. Finish this pattern.

    ◯ ◯

2. 4 **tens** 8 **units** = _____

3. Write the numeral sixty-seven.
   _____

4. 6 + 9 + 6 = _____

5. Fill in this section of the hundred square.

22	23		25
	33		35

6. Draw hands on the clock to show $\frac{1}{2}$ past 8.

7. 12, 14, 16, _____, 20, _____

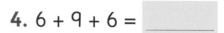

Vehicles that passed the school							
Cars	🚗	🚗	🚗	🚗	🚗	🚗	🚗	🚗
Vans	🚐	🚐	🚐	🚐	🚐			
Lorries	🚚	🚚	🚚	🚚	🚚	🚚		

8. How many cars passed by? _____

9. How many more lorries than vans passed by? _____

10. If half the lorries that passed by were red, how many red lorries passed by? _____

11. How many bananas are there altogether? _____

12. How many more are needed to have 50 bananas? _____

/12

Wednesday

1. Write the number shown on the abacus.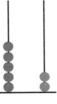

2. 39 + 31 = _____

3. 5 **tens** 4 **units** = _____

4. Draw the other half of this picture.

5. t u
   2 6
   −2 2
   _____

6. Draw hands on the clock to show $\frac{1}{2}$ past 3.

7. Colour half the triangle.

8. 17c = ◯ + ◯ + ◯

9. _____ , 54, 55, _____

10. A rectangle has _____ sides.

11. There were 36 apples in a box. 17 of them were bad. How many were good? _____

12. Jim had 86 cards. He gave 24 of them to Ellen. How many had he left? _____

/12

Thursday

1. Round 35 to the nearest 10. _____

2. My schoolbag weighs:
   ☐ more than 1kg.
   ☐ less than 1kg.
   ☐ about 1kg.

3. 7 **tens** 1 **unit** = _____

4. Add 10 to 49. _____

5. Show 39 on the abacus.

6. Draw hands on the clock to show $\frac{1}{2}$ past 12.

7. Colour half the circle.

8. 97, 98, _____ , 100

9. How many surfaces has a cuboid? _____

10. 26c = ◯ + ◯ + ◯

Maria is going to visit her aunt 6 days from today.

11. What day will that be? _____

12. Maria is 8 years old. Her aunt Anna is 39 years old. How much older is Anna than Maria? _____

/12

See page 73 for test.

Monday

1. What time is it?

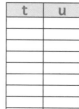

2. 7 + 4 + 3 = ____

t	u

3. Show 85 on the notation board.

4. 20c + ____ = 25c

5. Fill in the missing sign (<, >, =).
   20 − 5 ____ 3 + 11

6. Draw the missing coin to make a total of 42c.

7. t u
    3 5
   −2 4
   ____

8. In which season is June?
   ____

9. Colour half the semi-circle red.

10. 20, 22, 24, ____ , ____

11. Karl had 14 toys. Claire had 6 fewer. How many toys had Claire? ____

12. Catriona has 23 books. Adam has 12 more than Catriona. How many books has Adam? ____

/12

Tuesday

1. 4 + 4 + 4 = ____

2. What time is it? ____

3. Colour half the square.

4. Fill in the missing sign (<, >, =).
   31 ____ 25 + 7

5. In which season is December?
   ____

6. 43 + 10 = ____

7. 16 take away 8 = ____

8. Count the money. ____

9. Circle the container that can hold more water.

10. Draw a line of symmetry.

OCTOBER						
Mon	Tue	Wed	Thurs	Fri	Sat	Sun
			1	2	3	4
5	6	7	8	9	10	11
12	13	14	15	16	17	18
19	20	21	22	23	24	25
26	27	28	29	30	31	

11. How many Saturdays are there in October? ____

12. What date is the last Sunday in October? ____

/12

22

Wednesday

1. I eat my breakfast in the
   _____.
   (morning/afternoon/night)

2. 8 + 8 = _____

3. How many? _____

4. How many 5c coins make up 25c? _____

5. 12 subtract 6 = _____

6. Draw hands on the clock to show $\frac{1}{2}$ an hour earlier than 10 o'clock.

7. t u
     4 6
    − 3 1
    _____

8. What is the 7th month of the year? _____

9. Colour half of the set.

10. Draw two lines of symmetry.

11. What is the sum of seven and twelve? _____

12. There are 29 cars in a car park. 16 of them are red. The rest of the cars are black. How many cars are black? _____

/12

Thursday

1. I am in bed throughout the
   _____.
   (morning/afternoon/night)

2. 7 + 3 + 4 = _____

3. 12 − 0 = _____

4. How many? _____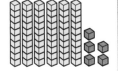

5. 8 plus 4 = _____

6. Draw hands on the clock to show one hour earlier than 12 o'clock.

7. Count the money.
   _____

8. In which season is March? _____

9. t u
     5 6
    − 1 1
    _____

10. Fill in the missing sign (<, >, =).
    4 + 5 _____ 10 − 3

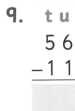 35c   30c   25c

11. How much does it cost to buy an apple and a pear? _____

12. How many oranges can I buy with 50c? _____

/12

See page 74 for test.

Monday

1. Draw a line of symmetry.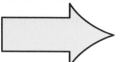

2. Your shoe is:
   ☐ more than 1 metre.
   ☐ less than 1 metre.
   ☐ about 1 metre.

3. $5 + 8 =$ _____

4. $12 -$ _____ $= 6$

5. $50c + 20c + 5c +$ _____ $= 80c$

6. $46 =$ _____ **tens** _____ **units**

7. Colour the even set **red**.

8. Share 8 bananas equally between 2 monkeys. Each monkey gets _____ bananas.

9. Colour the shape that can't roll.

10. Draw hands on the clock to show one hour earlier than $\frac{1}{2}$ past 1.

11. What must I add to 24 to make 48? _____

12. Luke has 4 punnets of strawberries. If there are 10 strawberries in each punnet, how many strawberries has Luke altogether? _____

/12

Tuesday

1. $9 + 4 =$ _____

2. This semi-circle is divided in half.
   ☐ Yes ☐ No

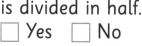

3. $6 + 6 +$ _____ $= 14$

4. Write the number shown on the abacus. _____

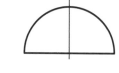

5. Write the numeral forty-seven. _____

6. How many faces has a cube? _____

7. Share 12 nuts equally between 2 squirrels. Each squirrel gets _____ nuts.

8. Write the numbers between 46 and 52. _____

9. Round 26 to the nearest 10. _____

10. A teaspoon holds:
    ☐ more than 1 litre.
    ☐ less than 1 litre.
    ☐ about 1 litre.

11. What do the cat and dog weigh together? _____

4kg   22kg

12. What is the difference in weight between the two animals? _____

/12

Wednesday

1. 8 add 9 = _____

2. 50 + 8 = _____

3. How many cubes are needed to balance the cup? _____

4. 45c = ◯ ◯ ◯

5. It is _____.

6. We measure milk in:
   - ☐ litres.
   - ☐ kilogrammes.
   - ☐ metres.

t	u

7. Show 67 on the notation board.

8. Colour the shape that can't roll.

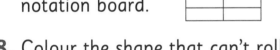

9. There are _____ days in a week.

10. Share 10 cars equally between 2 boys. Each boy gets _____ cars.

11. How many legs have four dogs and two birds? _____

12. Mammy went to town at 3 o'clock. She returned home at 5 o'clock. How long was she away? _____

/12

Thursday

1. Draw the other half of this picture.

2. 9 + 5 = _____

3. 10 + 10 + 10 + 10 = _____

4. Write the number shown on the abacus. _____

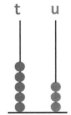

t   u

5. What fraction of this picture is not coloured? _____

6. 10 + _____ + 4 = 18

7. 30 – 10 = _____

8. How many months are in a year? _____

9. Write these numbers in order, starting with the smallest: 9, 5, 23, 78, 32.

_____ , _____ , _____ , _____ , _____

10. $\frac{1}{2}$ of _____ = 2

JULY						
Mon	Tue	Wed	Thurs	Fri	Sat	Sun
		1	2	3	4	5
6	7	8	9	10	11	12
13	14	15	16	17	18	19
20	21	22	23	24	25	26
27	28	29	30	31		

11. How many days are in July? _____

12. What day is a week from the 4th? _____

/12

See page 75 for test.

Monday

1. How many? _____

2. Fill in the missing numbers from this section of the hundred square.

	25	
34		
	45	

3. Circle the even number.

    11   19   15   16

4. Draw a line of symmetry.

5. $6 + 5$ _____ $4 + 2$ (<, >, =)

6. $44 - 10 =$ _____

7. Draw hands on the clock to show $\frac{1}{2}$ past 6.

8. Colour $\frac{1}{2}$ the flowers.

9. $24 - 12 =$ _____

10. $10c + 12c +$ _____ $= 30c$

11. Jason had 48 marbles. He lost 17 of them in a game. How many had he left? _____

12. Mammy gives Liam 20c every day he tidies his room. If Liam tidied his room on Monday, Tuesday and Wednesday, how much did he get? _____

/12

Tuesday

1. Write the number shown on the abacus. _____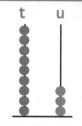

2. Fill in the missing numbers from this section of the hundred square.

18		
	29	
		40

3. Circle the odd number.

    14   21   22   26

4. Draw the other half of this picture.

5. $7 + 1$ _____ $9 + 1$ (<, >, =)

6. $63 + 21 =$ _____

7. What month is two months after February? _____

8. _____ is $\frac{1}{2}$ of 4.

9. $36 - 13 =$ _____

10. Your pencil weighs:
    ☐ less than 1kg.
    ☐ about 1kg.
    ☐ more than 1kg.

Today is Tuesday the 20th of May. Leah is having a party in 5 days' time.

11. On what day will Leah have her party on? _____

12. What date was it a week ago? _____

/12

Wednesday

1. Write the number shown on the notation board. _____

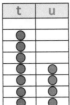

2. Take 7 from 12. _____

3. Circle the even number.

    55   42   69   85

4. Draw a line of symmetry.

5. 4 + 4 _____ 6 + 2 (<, >, =)

6. 49 – 11 = _____

7. Draw hands on the clock to show $\frac{1}{2}$ past 8.

8. Colour $\frac{1}{2}$ the set. _____ is $\frac{1}{2}$ of 10.

9. 69 + 10 = _____

10. A cup can hold:
    ☐ more than 1 litre.
    ☐ less than 1 litre.
    ☐ about 1 litre.

11. 41 girls and 36 boys were playing on the yard. How many children were on the yard altogether? _____

12. Patrick made 68 buns. He gave 25 to Sheila. How many had he then? _____

/12

Thursday

1. Show 49 on the abacus.

2. What day comes just after Friday? _____

3. Circle the odd number.

    12   45   36   86

4. Draw the other half of this picture.

5. 6 + 3 _____ 11 – 3 (<, >, =)

6. 76 + 13 = _____

7. _____ is the 4th month of the year.

8. Colour $\frac{1}{2}$ the set. _____ is $\frac{1}{2}$ of 12.

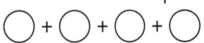

9. 57 – 17 = _____

10. What coins make up 36c?

    ◯ + ◯ + ◯ + ◯

Mammy is going to knit a jumper for each of her 5 children. Each jumper will have 4 buttons.

11. How many buttons will Mammy need? _____

12. Mammy bought a packet of 50 buttons. How many buttons will she have left over? _____

/12

See page 76 for test.

27

Monday

1. How many? **57**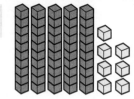

2. $9 + 6 = $ **15**

3. 12 subtract 5 = **7**

4. Circle the even number.

   23   45   53   (62)

5. Draw hands on the clock to show one hour earlier than 7 o'clock.

6. What do you see top left?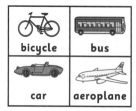

   bicycle

7. What do you see bottom right? _aeroplane_

8. Colour $\frac{1}{2}$ the set.

   8 is $\frac{1}{2}$ of **16** .

9. $24 - 12 = $ **12**

10. Double 10. **20**

11. Mark had 50c. He bought three buns at 10c each. How much change did he get? **20c**

12. Roisín had 42 stickers. She lost 12 and gave 5 to her friend. How many stickers does she have left? **34**

/12

Tuesday

1. Show 78 on the notation board.

t	u

2. 12 add 8 = _____

3. Fill in the missing numbers.

33	34		36
		45	
53			56

4. $4 + 5$ _____ $6 + 3$ (<, >, =)

5. What coins make up 47c?

   ○ + ○ + ○ + ○

6. Circle the lighter animal.

7. $20 - 9 = $ _____

8. Draw hands on the clock to show one hour later than 4 o'clock.

9. What do you see bottom left?

   _____

10. What do you see top right? _____

Chris counted the following insects in a field one day:
35 ladybirds, 28 ants and 23 butterflies.

11. How many insects altogether were there?

12. How many fewer butterflies than ladybirds were there?

/12

Wednesday

1. Draw the least number of coins needed to make 75c.

◯ ◯ ◯

2. 9 + 6 + ____ = 19

3.
```
 t u
 7 6
+1 8
____
```

4. Circle the odd number.

8   18   21   26

5. 40 + 50 = ____

6. Colour $\frac{1}{2}$ the set. ____ is $\frac{1}{2}$ of 16.

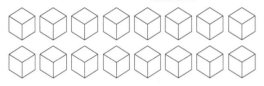

7. 10 + 3 ____ 20 − 8 (<, >, =)

8. 9 is half of ____.

9. Draw a line of symmetry.

10. 2, 4, 6, 8, ____

11. Mary had 3 pizzas. She cut each pizza into 4 slices. How many slices had she altogether? ____

12. John spent 10 minutes doing his maths homework, 5 minutes at his spellings and 5 minutes at his reading. How long did he spend doing his homework altogether?

____

/12

Thursday

1. Draw the least number of coins needed to make 90c.

◯ ◯ ◯

2. 3 + 6 + ____ = 15

3.
```
 t u
 8 8
−2 7
____
```

4. Circle the even number.

15   22   25   27

5. What month comes after February? _____

6. 4, 8, 12, ____, 20

7. How many? ____

8. How many surfaces has a sphere? ____

9. $\frac{1}{2}$ of ____ = 10

10. Draw the other half of this picture.

Shane spent 25c on an apple, 30c on a pear and 29c on a banana.

11. How much did he spend altogether? ____

12. How much less did the apple cost than the banana? ____

/12

See page 78 for test.

31

Monday

1. Draw the least number of coins needed to make 72c.

2. 5 + 2 + ____ = 12

3. How many? ____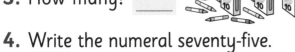

4. Write the numeral seventy-five.

   ____

5. 28 + 8 = ____

6. Match.

   sixth •   • 8th

   tenth •   • 6th

   eighth •   • 10th

7. 112 = ____ hundred

   ____ ten(s) ____ units

8. What month comes just after July? ____

9. Draw hands on the clock to show $\frac{1}{2}$ an hour later than 9 o'clock.

10. A football is the same shape as which 3-D shape? ____

11. Kevin has 27 grapes. Linda has 39. How many fewer grapes has Kevin than Linda? ____

12. Lisa swam 25 lengths of the pool. Tommy swam 23 lengths and Emma swam 8 lengths. How many lengths did they swim altogether? ____

/12

Tuesday

1. 5, 10, 15, ____, ____

2. Add 10 to 29. ____

3. 16 − 4 = ____

4. Draw hands on the clock to show $\frac{1}{2}$ an hour earlier than 6 o'clock.

5. Draw the least number of coins needed to make 85c.

6. Which is lighter, a bag full of (a) bricks or (b) feathers? ____

7. 38 + 12 = ____

8. 109 = ____ hundred

   ____ tens ____ units

Look at the bar chart and answer the following questions.

9. Which colour is most popular? ____

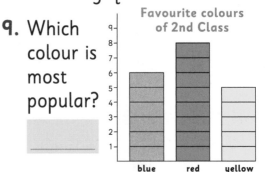

Favourite colours of 2nd Class

blue   red   yellow

10. Which colour is least popular? ____

11. How many children altogether in 2nd Class? ____

12. How many more children prefer red than yellow? ____

/12

Wednesday

1. 20, 18, 16, ____, ____

2. 15 – 6 = ____

3. What time is it?

_____

4. Draw a mirror image.

5. How many months in 1 year? ____

6. 4 + 7 + ____ = 18

7. 45 + 5 = ____

8. Colour $\frac{1}{2}$ the rectangle.

9. Write the numeral one hundred and twenty-five. ____

10. Tick the shape that would best cover your desk without leaving any gaps.

11. There are 52 cards in a deck. I have 21 cards. How many cards am I missing to make a deck? ____

12. Jason had 46 stamps. His daddy gave him 33 more. How many stamps had he then? ____

/12

Thursday

1. 13 – 4 = ____

2. Draw hands on the clock to show $\frac{1}{2}$ an hour earlier than 2 o'clock.

3. 4 + 6 ____ 15 – 5 (<, >, =)

4. Show 125 on the abacus.

5. t u
    3 9
  +2 5
   ____

6. How many sides has a semi-circle? ____

7. In which season are the months June, July and August? ____

8. Share 12 strawberries equally between 2 girls. Each girl gets ____ strawberries.

9. 5 glasses hold the same amount as the jug. True or false? ____

10. Circle the digit in the hundreds place: 124.

11. How many red and blue marbles are in the bag? ____

12. How many marbles are in the bag altogether? ____

/12

Monday

1. 25 + 32 + 21 = _____

2. 16, 20, 24, 28, _____

3.
```
  t u
  6 6
+ 3 4
_____
```

4. 6 + 2 → 4 + _____

5. Write the number shown on the abacus. _____
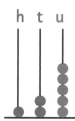

6. 7 + 9 _____ 14 − 3 (<, >, =)

7. Subtract 12 from 20. _____

8. Write these numbers in order, starting with the largest: 74, 18, 65, 30.
_____ , _____ , _____ , _____

9. 112 = _____ hundred _____ ten(s) _____ units

10. I am a 3-D shape. I have 1 curved face and 2 circular faces. I am a:

11. Liam bought 2 bags of flour for 25c each and 2 tins of soup for 20c each. How much change did he get back from €1? _____

12. Sharon found 8 horse chestnuts, Harry found 21 and Lisa found 19. How many horse chestnuts did they find altogether? _____

/12

Tuesday

1. How many does this tally show? _____

2. Write these numbers in order, starting with the smallest: 38, 17, 20, 32.
_____ , _____ , _____ , _____

3. 31 + 23 + 14 = _____

4. 99 + 17 = _____

5. 71 − _____ = 4

6. Write the number shown on the notation board. _____
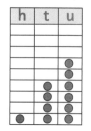

7. 7 + 6 _____ 17 − 8 (<, >, =)

8. Draw hands on the clock to show one hour later than $\frac{1}{2}$ past 11.

9. 18, 21, 24, 27, _____

10. How many sides has an oval? _____

11. I ate 2 slices of this pizza. How many slices are left? _____

12. If my sister ate half of what was left, how many slices are left then? _____

/12

Wednesday

1. Count the money. _____

2. 7, 17, 27, _____, 47

3. 56 – 42 = _____

4. 8 – 3 → 1 + _____

5. 11 + 26 + 22 = _____

6. What is the value of the underlined digit: 1̲25? _____

7. 14 + 7 _____ 25 – 6 (<, >, =)

8. Draw hands on the clock to show $\frac{1}{2}$ an hour past $\frac{1}{2}$ past 1.

9. Write these numbers in order, starting with the largest: 17, 14, 18, 20.
   _____, _____, _____, _____

10. Does this line show symmetry?
    ☐ Yes
    ☐ No

11. Peter bought 59 cards. He gave 27 away. How many had he left? _____

12. Mary eats 2 pieces of chocolate every day. How many pieces does she eat in a week (7 days)? _____

/12

Thursday

1. Draw the least number of coins needed to make 93c.

2. 10, 20, 30, _____

3. 21 + 36 + 12 = _____

4. What is the value of the underlined digit: 1̲3̲2? _____

5. How much change would I get from 50c if I bought an apple for 25c? _____

6. 74 – 10 = _____

7. 18 + 9 _____ 32 – 3 (<, >, =)

8. There are _____ months in a year.

9. Write these numbers in order, starting with the smallest: 15, 22, 16, 11.
   _____, _____, _____, _____

10. 18 – 3 → _____ + 9

3 glasses of water fill the jug.
2 jugs of water fill the kettle.

11. How many glasses will it take to fill 2 jugs? _____

12. How many jugs of water will it take to fill 3 kettles? _____

/12

See page 80 for test.

35

Monday

1. 3, 5, 7, _____ , _____

2. 6 add 5 = _____

3.
```
 t u
 3 5
-1 2
_____
```

h	t	u

4. Show 186 on the notation board.

5. What month comes just after August? _____

6. How many corners has a square? _____

7. What is the value of the underlined digit: 2<u>2</u>5? _____

8. Write these numbers in order, starting with the largest: 44, 39, 56, 24, 35.

_____ , _____ , _____ , _____ , _____

9. 35 + 43 + 1 = _____

10. Is this shape cut in quarters? ☐ Yes ☐ No

11. Jack bought a chocolate milkshake for 45c. Cian bought an orange juice for 52c. How much did the two drinks cost altogether? _____

12. How many fingers have four hands? _____

Tuesday

1. 13 – 4 = _____

2. 143 = _____ hundred _____ tens _____ units

3. Write the number shown on the abacus. _____

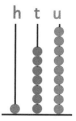

4. 4, 8, 12, _____ , _____

5. 8 + 6 = _____

6. Finish this pattern.

7. Draw hands on the clock to show $\frac{1}{2}$ past 2.

8. 23 + 11 + 15 = _____

9. 90 – 40 = _____

10. What is the month between October and December?

_____

There are 4 cars in a row. The red car is in front of the blue car. The green car is behind the yellow car. The green car is last. The blue car is in front of the yellow car.

11. Colour the cars.

12. How many wheels on the four cars? _____

Wednesday

1. 20, 16, 12, ____, ____

2. 7 plus 7 = ____

3. What is the value of the underlined digit: <u>1</u>38? ____

4. I have 6 rectangular faces. My opposite faces are equal. What 3-D shape am I?
   _____

5. 47 − 35 = ____

6. Colour $\frac{1}{4}$ of this shape.

7. What is the day between Tuesday and Thursday?
   _____

8. How much change will I get from 50c if I buy the book? ____

35c

9. How much longer is ruler (b) than ruler (a)? ____

   (a) _____ 10cm

   (b) _____ 12cm

10. $\frac{1}{2}$ of 10 = ____

11. Peter had 19 apples. He gave 12 of them to his teacher. How many had he left? ____

12. There were 28 people on the bus. 15 people got off the bus. 22 got on. How many were on the bus then? ____

/12

Thursday

1. Write the number shown on the abacus. ____

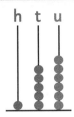

2. 4 + 4 + 4 = ____

3. 5 + 7 ____ 6 + 4 (<, >, =)

4. Draw hands on the clock to show one hour later than $\frac{1}{2}$ past 8.

5. Write these numbers in order, starting with the smallest: 12, 6, 32, 22, 52.
   ____, ____, ____, ____, ____

6. Colour $\frac{1}{4}$ of the bananas.

7. 42 − 12 = ____

8. _____ is the 1st month of the year.

9. Is this shape symmetrical? ____

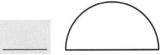

10. Two of my faces are circles. My third face is curved. What 3-D shape am I? _____

A petrol tank holds 50l, an oil tank holds 90l and a barrel holds 20l.

11. How many litres altogether do the barrel and petrol tank hold? ____

12. How many litres less does the barrel hold than the oil tank? ____

/12

See page 81 for test.

Monday

1. 7 add 7 = ____

2. 12 − 6 = ____

3. Share 6 crayons equally between 2 children. Each child gets ____ crayons.

4. Show 125 on the abacus.

h t u

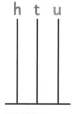

5. Measure this line. ____ cm

6. Colour $\frac{1}{4}$ of the ladybirds.

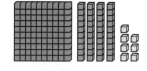

7. How many? ____

8. Count the money. ____

9. 30, 40, 50, ____, ____

10. 33 + 24 = ____

11. What must be added to 13 to make 26? ____

12. There are 14 children in the playground. $\frac{1}{2}$ of them are wearing runners. How many are wearing runners? ____

/12

Tuesday

1. What time is it? _____

2. 15 − 7 = ____

MARCH						
Mon	Tue	Wed	Thurs	Fri	Sat	Sun
						1
2	3	4	5	6	7	8
9	10	11	12	13	14	15
16	17	18	19	20	21	22
23	24	25	26	27	28	29
30	31					

3. How many Tuesdays are in March? ____

4. Write the date of each Friday. ____, ____, ____, ____

5. On what day does the 18th fall? _____

6. How many lines of symmetry has a square? ____

7. How many 5c coins make up 50c? ____

8. Write one hundred and twenty-six as a numeral. ____

9. How long is the pencil? ____ cm

10. Circle the odd number.

12   16   15   18

11. I ate $\frac{1}{2}$ of the pizza. How many slices are left? ____

12. Then Noah ate 2 of the remaining slices. What fraction of the whole pizza did he eat? ____

/12

Wednesday

1. 5 + 9 + 12 = ____

2. 16 take away 4 = ____

3. How many crayons? ____

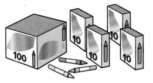

4. Draw a mirror image.

5. How many wheels are on three bicycles? ____

6. Circle the even number.

   5   12   13   15

7. My pencil case weighs:

   ☐ more than 1kg.

   ☐ less than 1kg.

   ☐ about 1kg.

8. 33 + 24 = ____

9. Make up 80c using the least number of coins possible.

10. Fill in the missing numbers.

	18		20
27		29	
		39	40

11. Seán had 24 sweets. He gave 14 sweets to his brother. How many had he left? ____

12. Lisa went for a walk at 3 o'clock. She got back at $\frac{1}{2}$ past 3. How long did she spend walking? ____

/12

Thursday

1. 15, 12, 9, ____, ____

2. How many days in a week? ____

3. How many lines of symmetry can you draw through this shape? ____

4. Which comes first during the day: sunrise, midday or sunset? ____

5. 5 + 6 + ____ = 14

6.   t u
     3 5
   − 2 3
     ____

7. 3 + 3 + 3 + 3 = ____

8. 30 + 10 + 5 = ____

9. What fraction of this shape is coloured? ____

10. Measure this line. ____ cm

2nd Class – Favourite sport

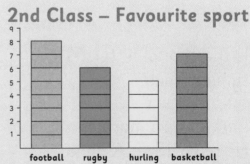

11. How many children altogether prefer basketball and rugby? ____

12. How many children are in this 2nd Class? ____

/12

See page 82 for test.

Monday

1. 6, 12, _____, 24, 30

2. 3 + 5 + 5 = _____

3. $\frac{1}{2}$ of 8 = _____

4. How many corners has a cube? _____

5. How long is the straw? _____ cm

6. Draw hands on the clock to show 1 hour earlier than $\frac{1}{2}$ past 9.

7. How many days in May? _____

MAY						
Mon	Tue	Wed	Thurs	Fri	Sat	Sun
27	28	29	30	1	2	3
4	5	6	7	8	9	10
11	12	13	14	15	16	17
18	19	20	21	22	23	24
25	26	27	28	29	30	31

8. What date is the last Friday in May? _____

9. What day is the 19th of May? _____

10. Is the capital letter **M** symmetrical? _____

11. Ben had 46 marbles. He gave 13 to Alanna. How many has he left? _____

12. Alice bought an ice-cream cone for 36c. How much would 2 ice-cream cones cost? _____

/12

Tuesday

1. Show 163 on the abacus.

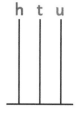

2. Tick the shapes that are $\frac{1}{4}$ coloured.

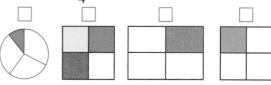

3. Is 57 closer to 50 or 60? _____

4. 30 + 40 = _____

5.
```
 t u
 4 6
+3 4
─────
```
_____

6. How many cubes balance the cup? _____

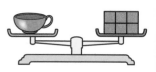

7. 7 + 7 + 7 = _____

8. Measure this line. _____ cm

9. $\frac{1}{2}$ of 24 = _____

10. 67 – 10 _____ 56 + 5 (<, >, =)

11. I read 21 pages of my book on Monday and 34 on Tuesday. How many pages did I read altogether? _____

96 pages

12. How many pages of my book have I left to read? _____

/12

Wednesday

1. 5 + 7 + 2 = _____

2. 4, 8, 12, _____, _____

3. How many 10c coins make up €1? _____

4. 60 + 10 + 3 = _____

5. Draw hands on the clock to show $\frac{1}{2}$ an hour later than 5 o'clock.

6. How many edges has a cube? _____

7. How many centimetres in a metre? ☐ 10 ☐ 100 ☐ 1,000

8. $\frac{1}{2}$ of 10 = _____

9. Colour $\frac{1}{4}$ of the marbles.

10. Name this shape. _____

11. 28 birds were sitting on a tree. More birds came and landed on the same tree. Then there were 40 birds. How many more flew up to the tree? _____

12. Hannah had a piece of string measuring 38cm. Jake had a piece measuring 15cm longer than Hannah's. What was the length of Jake's piece of string? _____

/12

Thursday

1. 15 take away 6 = _____

2. Count the money. _____

3. Draw hands on the clock to show an hour later than $\frac{1}{2}$ past 12.

4. How many edges has a cuboid? _____

5. Colour $\frac{1}{4}$ of this shape.

6. 7 is $\frac{1}{2}$ of _____.

7. Today is Monday. Tomorrow is _____.

8. Which bird is heavier? _____
(a)   (b)
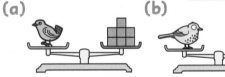

9. 10, 12, 14, _____, 18, _____

10.
```
  t u
  5 7
+ 2 4
_____
```

11. How many legs have the dogs and birds altogether? _____

12. How many eyes have the dogs and cats altogether? _____

/12

See page 83 for test.

Monday

1. How many faces has a cube? _____

2. $65 - 9 =$ _____

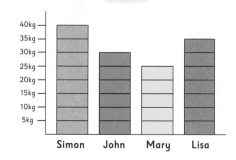

| | Simon | John | Mary | Lisa |

3. Who is the heaviest? _____

4. Who is the lightest? _____

5. How much heavier is Lisa than John? _____

6. How much do the children weigh altogether? _____

7. $\frac{1}{4}$ of 24 = _____

8. Colour $\frac{1}{2}$ the rectangle.

9. Measure this line. _____ cm

10. Draw a line of symmetry.

11. Andrew had €1. He gave $\frac{1}{4}$ of his money to Louise. How much did Andrew have left? _____

12. Jenny wrote the number 46 instead of 64. By how much was her answer too small? _____

/12

Tuesday

1. What 3-D shape can roll, slide and stack? _____

2. $6 + 2 + 1 \rightarrow 15 -$ _____

3. How many centimetres in a metre? _____

4. $\frac{1}{2}$ of 20 = _____

5. How long is this crayon? _____

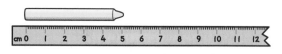

6. $14 + 13 + 22 =$ _____

7. Draw the other half of this picture.

8. 6, 12, 18, 24, _____

9. How many? _____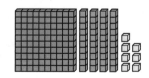

10. $14 +$ _____ $= 22$

Mammy decides to knit gloves and socks for her 3 children. It takes two balls of wool to make gloves and socks for 1 child.

11. How many balls of wool will Mammy need to make gloves and socks for the children? _____

12. If each ball of wool costs €2, how much will it cost to make all the gloves and socks? _____

/12

42

Wednesday

1. How many corners has a cuboid? _____

2.
```
   t u
   9 8
  -2 6
  ____
```

3. Draw hands on the clock to show half an hour earlier than 6 o'clock.

4. $\frac{1}{4}$ of 28 = _____

5. A bucket holds:
   - ☐ more than 1kg.
   - ☐ less than 1kg.
   - ☐ about 1kg.

6. A rectangle has _____ corners.

7. 12 + 16 + 21 = _____

8. How long is the carrot? _____ cm

9. How many? _____

10. 17 + _____ = 24

11. Emer had 75 stamps. She sold 42 of them. How many had she left? _____

12. Patrick had 8 strawberries. He ate $\frac{1}{2}$ of them. How many did he eat? _____

/12

Thursday

1. Draw the next shape in the pattern.

 _____

2. 72 – 40 = _____

3. Draw hands on the clock to show half an hour later than 11 o'clock.

4. $\frac{1}{2}$ of 12 = _____

5. €1 + 50c + 20c = _____

6. How many sides has a square? _____

7. 22 + 14 + 32 = _____

8. 8, 16, 24, 32, _____

9. How many? _____

10. 23 + _____ = 30

11. Write these weights in order of size, starting with the lightest:
    _____, _____, _____.

12. Which of the weights will balance these scales? _____

/12

See page 84 for test.

Monday

1. How many sides has a rectangle? _____

2. $\frac{1}{2}$ of 6 = _____

3. Draw a line of symmetry.

4. t u
    8 6
   –2 4
   _____

5. 8 + 9 + _____ = 22

6. The 6th month of the year is _____.

7. 11 + 14 + 23 = _____

8. Draw the least number of coins needed to make 77c.

   ◯ ◯ ◯ ◯

9. 7, 14, 21, 28, _____

10. Colour the cone.

11. Jason had 20c. He spent half his money on stickers. How much had he left? _____

12. There were 23 people on a bus. At the bus stop, 21 people got off and 18 got on. How many were on the bus then? _____

/12

Tuesday

1. 50 + _____ = 58

2. 6 + 4 + 3 → 3 + 4 + _____

3. Circle the digit in the units place: 175.

4. Colour the shape that can roll.

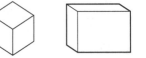

5. 9 + _____ + 6 = 22

6. 25 + 30 = _____

7. Mary had: How many more cent did she need to have €1? _____

8. 9 + 9 + 1 = _____

9. What is the value of the underlined digit: 1̲19? _____

10. How many months in summer and autumn altogether? _____

The farmer collected 35 eggs from his hens one morning.

11. He sold 12 and broke 7. How many eggs did he have left? _____

12. If he collected 21 eggs the next day, how many eggs did the farmer have then? _____

/12

44

Wednesday

1. How many sides has a triangle?

2. $\frac{1}{2}$ of 8 = _____

3. Draw a line of symmetry.

4.
```
  t u
  4 5
− 1 4
─────
_____
```

5. What time is it? _____

6. July is in the season of _____.

7. 13 + 25 + 21 = _____

8. Draw the least number of coins needed to make 85c.

9. 10, 20, 30, 40, _____

10. How many faces has a cone? _____

11. Mark wrote down the number 45. Jill wrote down a number 28 greater than that. What number did Jill write down? _____

12. Sarah spent half of her 22c buying a pencil. How much was the pencil? _____

/12

Thursday

1. 41 + _____ = 50

2. 9 + 1 + 6 → 6 + 1 + _____

3. Circle the digit in the tens place: 766.

4. Colour the oval.

5. 8 + _____ + 3 = 15

6. Write the number shown on the abacus. _____

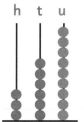

7. Pete has:

How much more does he need to have 65c? _____

8. 10 + 8 + 2 → 10 + _____

9. What is the value of the underlined digit: 14<u>7</u>? _____

10. How many minutes in 1 hour? _____

There are 8 cows and 2 sheep in a field.

11. How many legs have the cows and sheep altogether? _____

12. How many eyes have the cows and sheep altogether? _____

/12

See page 85 for test.

Monday

1. 60 + ___ = 69

2. 7 + 5 + 8 → 8 + 5 + ___

3. Circle the digit in the hundreds place: 166.

4. Colour the shape that cannot stack.

5. 7 + ___ + 6 = 20

6.
```
 t u
 3 8
+2 9
____
```

7. What time is it?

___ to ___

8. 4 + 4 + 1 → 5 + ___ + 1

9. 11, 22, 33, 44, ___

10. How many months are there in a year and a half? ___

11. Ben has:

How much change did he get when he bought the apple? ___

35c

12. 47 girls and 29 boys were in the yard. How many children were in the yard altogether? ___

/12

Tuesday

1. What time is it?

___ past ___

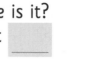

2. Draw the other half of this picture.

3.
```
 t u
 7 3
+2 1
____
```

4. ¼ of 8 = ___

5. Show 149 on the abacus.

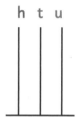

6. 4 + ___ = 12

7. 22 + 21 + 14 = ___

8. Draw the least number of coins needed to make 74c.

9. 6, 12, 18, ___, 30

10. Name a 3-D shape that can roll.

___

Anita has 3 lollies, Grace has 5 lollies and Jack has 4 lollies.

11. They decided to share their lollies equally between them. How many did each get? ___

12. If Mammy gave them 6 more lollies, how many would they have altogether? ___

/12

46

Wednesday

1. $140 + \underline{\hspace{1cm}} = 170$

2. What 3-D shape is this?

3. What fraction is coloured?

4. What is $\frac{1}{2}$ of 18? _____

Children's birthdays

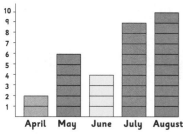

5. Which month has the most birthdays? _____

6. Which month has the least birthdays? _____

7. How many more children were born in August than in June? _____

8. What is the 3rd month of the year? _____

9. Draw hands on the clock to show $\frac{1}{4}$ to 4.

10. $64c + \underline{\hspace{1cm}} = €1$

11. A farmer had 62 cattle. He sold 23 of them. How many had he left? _____

12. Brian had 34 marbles, Theo had 12 and Louise had 10. How many marbles did they have altogether? _____

/12

Thursday

1. How many corners has a triangle? _____

2. $\frac{1}{4}$ of 4 = _____

3. Draw the other half of this picture.

4.
```
  t u
  6 7
+ 2 4
_____
```

5. Draw hands on the clock to show $\frac{1}{4}$ past 12.

6. $8 + \underline{\hspace{1cm}} = 20$

7. $14 + 21 + 22 = \underline{\hspace{1cm}}$

8. Draw the least number of coins needed to make 58c.

9. 4, 8, 12, _____, 20

10. How many faces has a cuboid? _____

There are 58 oranges and 34 apples in a box.

11. How many more oranges than apples are in the box? _____

12. If I took half the oranges and half the apples out of the box, how many pieces of fruit are left in the box? _____

/12

See page 86 for test.

Monday

1. Draw the least number of coins needed to make 45c.

   ◯ ◯ ◯

2. $6 + 3 + \underline{} = 15$

3. How many straws? $\underline{}$

   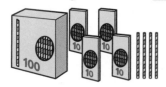

4. How many right angles has a square? $\underline{}$

5. $21 + 17 = \underline{}$

6. Match.

   fourth • • 10th
   ninth • • 4th
   tenth • • 9th

7. $12 + 12 + 12 + 12 = \underline{}$

8. The last month of the year is $\underline{}$.

9. Write the time 5 o'clock in digital form. ☐ : ☐

10. What 2-D shape is my pencil case? $\underline{}$

11. There were 21 frogs in a pond. If 9 frogs left the pond, how many frogs would be left? $\underline{}$

12. A piece of rope was 74m long. Jack cut off 32m. What length of rope is left in metres? $\underline{}$

/12

Tuesday

1. 4, 8, 12, $\underline{}$, $\underline{}$

2. How many right angles has a rectangle? $\underline{}$

3. $19 - 7 = \underline{}$

4. Write the time $\frac{1}{2}$ past 10 in digital form. ☐ : ☐

5. How many cents in €1·53? $\underline{}$

6. Tick the lighter bag.

   Potatoes   Leaves

   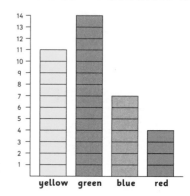

   ☐   ☐

7. $39 + 20 = \underline{}$

8. Colour $\frac{1}{4}$ of the apples.

   ◯ ◯ ◯ ◯ ◯ ◯ ◯ ◯

Look at the graph below.

2nd Class – Favourite colours

(bar graph: yellow = 11, green = 14, blue = 7, red = 4)

9. Which is the most popular colour? $\underline{}$

10. Which is the least popular? $\underline{}$

11. How many children are in the class? $\underline{}$

12. How many more children prefer green than red? $\underline{}$

/12

Wednesday

1. 2, 4, 6, ____, ____

2. Add 10 to 59. ____

3. 17 – 9 = ____

4. Write the time $\frac{1}{2}$ past 4 in digital form. [__ : __]

5. How many 5c coins in 50c? ____

6. Tick the heavier animal.

 ☐    ☐

7. 36 + 20 = ____

8. Colour $\frac{1}{2}$ of the carrots.

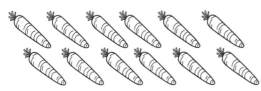

9. Circle the number that does not belong

   19   17   21   20

10. Write these numbers in order, starting with the smallest: 41, 48, 42, 40.

____, ____, ____, ____

11. What is the total weight of these 3 suitcases? ____

12. A window is 45cm wide. How wide are two windows? ____

/12

Thursday

1. Is this a right angle?
☐ Yes ☐ No

2. Write these numbers in order, starting with the largest: 31, 29, 21, 23.

____, ____, ____, ____

3. 120, 140, ____, 180

4. 1 **hundred** + 5 **tens** + 4 **units** = ____

5. $\frac{1}{4}$ of 12 = ____

6. Circle the smallest amount.
€2·03 50c 40c €1·10

7. 93 – 50 = ____

8. 30c + 30c + 20c = ____

9. Write the time $\frac{1}{2}$ past 9 in digital form. [__ : __]

10. Tick the lightest object.

 ☐   ☐   ☐

There were two horse chestnut trees. One had 42 horse chestnuts and the other had 55.

11. How many horse chestnuts did the two trees have altogether? ____

12. If wind blew 22 horse chestnuts off the trees, how many did the two trees have left? ____

/12

See page 87 for test.

Monday

1. How many $\frac{1}{2}$kg make a kilogramme? ____

2. 6 + 8 + ____ = 17

3. Finish the pattern.

   ____

4. 68 – 15 = ____

5. How many faces has a cone? ____

6. Write the time shown on the clock. [:]

7. t u
     3 8
   +4 3
   ____

8. 4 + ____ = 37

9. 22 + 22 + 1 → 40 + ____

10. This angle is:
    ☐ bigger than a right angle.
    ☐ smaller than a right angle.

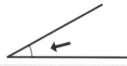

11. A football match started at 5 o'clock. It lasted 60 minutes. At what time did it finish? [:]

12. Hannah has 30c. She has 10c more than Lily. How much has Lily? ____

/12

50

Tuesday

1. Which is heavier, a $\frac{1}{2}$kg or a $\frac{1}{4}$kg? ____

2. Measure this line. ____ cm

_____

3. 9 + 7 + ____ = 19

4. 79 – 27 = ____

5. 31 + 31 + 1 → 60 + ____

6. Draw a 3-D shape that rolls.

7. How many sides has a semi-circle? ____

8. How long does it take the long hand to make a complete turn? ____

9. How many edges has a sphere? ____

10. How much change would I get from €1 if I bought this ruler?

____

 **50c**

11. Pete had a basketball match. It started at **2:30** and finished at half past 3. How many minutes did it last for? ____

12. Pete arrived home at 4 o'clock. He went to bed at 10 o'clock. How long is it from 4 o'clock to 10 o'clock? ____

/12

Wednesday

1. Colour the shape that can stack.

2. Divide this circle in half. How many parts did you get? _____

3. What angle does a $\frac{1}{4}$ turn in a circle make?

_____

4. 10, 12, 14, ____ , ____

5. How many $\frac{1}{4}$ kg make a kilogramme? _____

6. 49 – 23 = _____

7. 31, 33, 35, ____ , ____

8. How many wheels on 4 cars? _____

9. What is 4 more than 36? _____

10. How many toes have 3 people?

_____

11. If Jan ran 4 metres and Ivan ran 13 metres, how far did they run altogether? _____

12. If it takes 4 eggs to make a cake, how many eggs do you need to make 5 cakes? _____

/12

Thursday

1. How much longer is the blue straw than the red straw? _____

2. How many eggs are there? _____

3. Which is lighter, 1kg or three $\frac{1}{4}$ kg? _____

4. Subtract 6 from 66. _____

5. Write one hundred and forty-two as a numeral. _____

6. Count the money. _____

7. Circle the digit in the units place: 182.

8. How many minutes are in $2\frac{1}{2}$ hours? _____

9. Write the time half past 7 in digital form. [:]

10. There are _____ centimetres in a metre.

26c   40c   32c

11. How much do the whistle, yo-yo and die cost altogether? _____

12. How much change would I get from €1 if I bought all three items? _____

/12

See page 88 for test.

Monday

1. What is the weight of the box?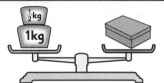

   _____

2. 37 + 42 = _____

3. 78 – 40 = _____

4. Tick the right angles in this shape.

5. How many legs have 4 horses?

   _____

6. Add these coins and write the answer using the euro sign.

   _____

7. I have 20c. How much more do I need to buy the pen?

   €1·25

   _____

8. 7 **tens** and 6 **units** =
   6 **tens** and _____ **units**

9. What time is it one hour earlier than the time shown?

   [:]

10. How many eggs in 7 trays, if there are 6 eggs in a tray?

    _____

11. Paul has 16 books. Shona has 19 books. How many more books do they need to have 40 books altogether? _____

12. Today is the 7th of May. What date was it 5 days ago? _____

/12

Tuesday

1. What is the weight of one bottle? ½ kg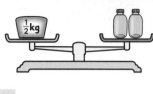

2. 64 + 22 = 86

3. 69 – 31 = 38

4. Tick the right angle in this shape.

5. How many legs have 6 ducks? 12

6. Add these coins and write the answer using the euro sign.

   £1 35c

7. 4 **tens** and 5 **units** = you are
   3 **tens** and 15 **units** dum!

8. What time is it one hour later than the time shown? 8:00

9. Measure this line. 3 cm
   1 2 3

10. How much change will I get from €2 if I spend 89c? £1 11c

Brian has €2.   70c

11. What is the greatest number of caps Brian can buy with €2? 2

12. How much change would Brian get if he bought as many caps as he could with €2? 60

/12

52

Wednesday

1. What is the weight of two tins? 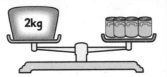 ____

2. 75 + 14 = ____

3. 79 − 11 = ____

4. Put a ✓ in the circle if it is a right angle and an ✗ if it is not.

5. How many legs have 3 lions? ____

6. 101, 102, 103, ____, 105

7. 6 **tens** and 8 **units** = 5 **tens** and ____ **units**

8. What time is it 2 hours earlier than the time shown? [:]

9. How many bags of sugar make 5kg? ____

10. How much change will I get from €3 if I spend €1·50? ____

11. There are 5 people in a queue at the cinema. If they all pay €4, how much will they pay in total? ____

12. The baker uses 4 eggs to make a cake. How many cakes did he make with 20 eggs? ____

/12

Thursday

1. Two of which weight balance the 1kg weight: $\frac{1}{4}$kg or $\frac{1}{2}$kg?  ____

2. 25 + 64 = ____

3. 79 − 23 = ____

4. How many balloons are there? ____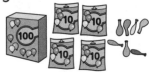

5. How many eyes have eight owls? ____

6. Add these coins and write the answer using the euro sign. ____

7. 7 **tens** and 4 **units** = 6 **tens** and ____ **units**

8. What time is it 2 hours later than the time shown? [:]

9. How many bags of flour add up to 4kg? ____

10. 9 + 9 + 9 + 9 = ____

32 boys and 36 girls were playing on the yard.

11. How many children were on the yard altogether? ____

12. Half the boys and one quarter of the girls went inside. How many children were left on the yard? ____

/12

See page 89 for test.

Monday

1. Fill in the missing numbers on this section of the hundred square.

13		15	
	24		26

2. Write the time $\frac{1}{2}$ past 10 in digital form. [:]

3. Colour $\frac{1}{4}$ of the buttons.

4. 23 + 16 + 20 = _____

5. Can this cup hold more or less than a litre? _____

6. 17, 20, 23, _____, 29

7. 20 is $\frac{1}{2}$ of _____.

8. How much shorter is straw (a) than straw (b)? _____

(a) _____ 10cm
(b) _____ 12cm

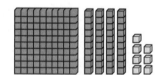

9. 76 – 10 = _____

10. How many cubes? _____

11. A programme started at 5 o'clock and finished at **6:30**. How long did it last?

_____

12. If a $\frac{1}{4}$-litre of water costs 30c, how much for 2 litres? _____

/12

Tuesday

1. Fill in the missing numbers on this section of the hundred square.

27		29	
	38		40

2. t u
    4 6
   –2 9
   _____

3. Write the time 7 o'clock in digital form. [:]

4. 41 + 14 + 24 = _____

5. Can this bucket hold more or less than a litre? _____

6. 30 is $\frac{1}{2}$ of _____.

7. 16, 18, 20, _____, 24

h	t	u

8. Show 173 on the notation board.

9. How many edges has a cone? _____

10. (8 + 6) – 9 = _____

1kg $\frac{1}{2}$ kg $\frac{1}{4}$ kg

11. How many nets of oranges will balance the apples? _____

12. How many punnets of strawberries will balance the net of oranges? _____

/12

54

Wednesday

1. Fill in the missing numbers on this section of the hundred square.

51		53	
	62		64

2. Write the time half past 8 in digital form. ☐ : ☐

3. 32, 34, ____, 38, 40

4. 16 + 21 + 42 = ____

Favourite sport

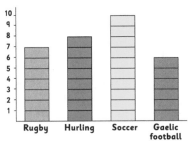

5. Which sport is the most popular? ____

6. Which sport is the least popular? ____

7. How many pupils took part in the survey? ____

8. 15 is $\frac{1}{2}$ of ____.

9. 68 – 17 = ____

10. I have 50c. I spent half. How much have I left? ____

11. Daddy was walking from 4 o'clock until half past 5. How long was that? ____

12. A farmer had 8 white cows and 9 black cows. She sold 3. How many has she left? ____

/12

Thursday

1. Fill in the missing numbers on this section of the hundred square.

47		49	
	58		60

2. Write the time 2 o'clock in digital form. ☐ : ☐

3. Show 166 on the notation board.

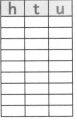

h	t	u

4. 12 + 41 + 64 = ____

5. I spent half of my 80c. How much have I left? ____

6. 24, 27, 30, ____, 36

7. 74 – 32 = ____

8. 25 is $\frac{1}{2}$ of ____.

9. 8 **tens** and 4 **units** = 7 **tens** and ____ **units**

10. How many wheels are on 4 bicycles? ____

A squirrel stored 27 acorns and 19 chestnuts.

11. How many nuts in total is that? ____

12. If the squirrel lost 15 of these nuts, how many did he have left? ____

/12

See page 90 for test.

Monday

1. Write the correct number.

h	t	u

2. What number is bigger than 37 by 30? ____

3. A match began at 3 o'clock. It lasted for 2 hours. At what time did it finish? [:]

4. How many $\frac{1}{4}$ litres in 1 litre? ____

5. 50c + 10c + ____ = €1

6. $\frac{1}{4}$ of 24 + $\frac{1}{2}$ of 12 = ____

7. How many minutes in half an hour? ____

8. 7, 14, 21, ____

9. Colour the shape that is symmetrical.

10.
```
 t u
 9 3
-7 8
────
```

11. In a race of 21 horses, Sea King finished in the middle. What place did she finish in? ____

12. If $\frac{1}{4}$ kg of flour costs 40c, how much would 1kg cost? ____

/12

Tuesday

1. Show 190 on the abacus.

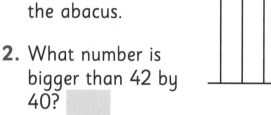

2. What number is bigger than 42 by 40? ____

3. A school opened at 9 o'clock. Playtime was 2 hours later. What time was that? [:]

4. How much? ____

5. How much change would I get from €2 if I bought 2 balls? ____

6. $\frac{1}{2}$ of 18 + $\frac{1}{4}$ of 16 = ____

7. How many minutes in $2\frac{1}{2}$ hours? ____

8. 8, 16, 24, ____

9. Colour the shape that is not symmetrical.

10. 47 − 32 = ____

11. How many bottles of tomato sauce would fill the bottle of orange? ____

12. How many tins of soup would fill the bottle of tomato sauce? ____

/12

Wednesday

1. Show 124 on the abacus.

 h t u

2. What number is bigger than 64 by 20? _____

3. A film began at $\frac{1}{2}$ past 9. It finished at 11 o'clock. How long did it last? _____

4. How much? _____

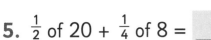

5. $\frac{1}{2}$ of 20 + $\frac{1}{4}$ of 8 = _____

6. How many minutes in an hour? _____

7. Which has the larger area, (a) or (b) ? _____

(a) ☐   (b) ☐

8. Circle the letter that is symmetrical. **F   G   L   M**

9. 94 − 61 = _____

10. How many litres are there? _____

11. Fran climbed 8 steps and then 6 more. He came down 2. What step was he on then? _____

12. Nadia wrote the number 51 instead of 79. By how much was her answer too small? _____

/12

Thursday

1. Write the number shown on the abacus. _____

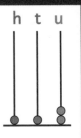 h t u

2. 11, 18, 25, _____

3. What number is smaller than 64 by 10? _____

4. What time is one hour before **2:30** ? [:]

5. How many litres are there? _____

6. 15 + 16 + _____ = 35

7. How much for an apple and a banana? _____

 32c 17c

8. How many days in 3 weeks? _____

9. Divide this circle in quarters.

10. t u
    4 7
   −2 8
    _____

 €1·35   55c

11. How much more expensive is the book than the rubber? _____

12. Jack had €2. He bought the book for €1·35. How much change did he get back? _____

/12

See page 91 for test.

Monday

1. How many glasses can be filled with water from the jug?
_____

2. What is the area of this shape in small squares? _____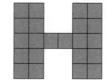

3. 43 − 8 = _____

4. Write the value of:
_____

5. I have 80c. How much more do I need to have €2? _____

6. Conor's birthday is in January. Becky's birthday is in April. How many months later is Becky's birthday? _____

7. 7, 14, 21, _____

8. Yuri has twelve 10c coins. How much is that in total? _____

9. Write $\frac{1}{2}$ past 7 in digital time. [:]

10. Draw a line of symmetry.

11. Cian is collecting stickers. He has 76. How many more does he need to have 90? _____

12. The dog ate half the bones and there are 7 left. How many bones in total were there? _____

/12

Tuesday

1. 7 **tens** and 4 **units** = 6 **tens** and _____ **units**

2. A camogie match started at $\frac{1}{2}$ past 2. If it lasted $\frac{1}{2}$ an hour, at what time did it finish? [:]

3. 72 − 12 = _____

4. Draw a line of symmetry.

5. 14 + 12 + _____ = 34

6. I have 75c. How much more do I need to have €2? _____

7. Measure this line. _____ cm

8. Finish the pattern.

9. 7 + 7 + 7 = _____

10. (14 + 8) − 3 = _____

Vehicles that passed the school																	
Cars	🚗	🚗	🚗	🚗	🚗	🚗	🚗	🚗	🚗	🚗	🚗	🚗	🚗	🚗			
Vans	🚐	🚐	🚐	🚐	🚐	🚐	🚐	🚐	🚐	🚐							
Lorries	🚚																
Motorbikes	🏍	🏍	🏍														

11. What is the difference between the number of cars and the number of lorries that passed the school? _____

12. How many vehicles in total passed the school? _____

/12

58

Wednesday

1. 6 **tens** and 4 **units** =
   5 **tens** and ___ **units**

2. How many faces has a cone? ___

3. How much taller is
   flower (a) than
   flower (b)? ___

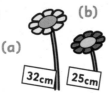
(b)
(a)
32cm 25cm

4. 26 − 15 = ___

5. Write the value of:

___

6. I had €2. I spent 20c and €1·10.
   How much change
   did I get back? ___

7. Write $\frac{1}{2}$ past 6
   in digital time. [:]

8. I have two circular faces and
   one curved face. What 3-D
   shape am I? ___

9. $\frac{1}{4}$kg ___ $\frac{1}{2}$kg (<, >, =)

10. Tick the right angle.

11. Joan ate 10 grapes over three
    days. She ate 2 on Monday and
    3 on Tuesday. How many did
    she eat on Wednesday? ___

12. I had €2. I spent 10c in one shop
    and 75c in another shop.
    How much do I have left? ___

/12

Thursday

1. 9 **tens** and 3 **units** =
   8 **tens** and ___ **units**

2. 34 − 22 = ___

3. (16 + ___) − 4 = 22

4. I have 80c. How much more do
   I need to have €2? ___

Favourite fruit

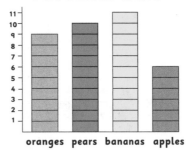

oranges pears bananas apples

5. Which fruit is
   the most popular? ___

6. Which fruit is
   the least popular? ___

7. How many children took part in
   the survey? ___

8. Write $\frac{1}{2}$ past 4 in
   digital time. [:]

9. Colour two quarters
   of the rectangle. [ ]

10. How many centimetres
    in $\frac{1}{4}$ of a metre? ___

Peter has 10c, Jack has 5c and
Joe has 6c.

11. The three children shared their
    money equally.
    How much did each get? ___

12. If they had 3c more in total,
    how much would each get then?
    ___

/12

See page 92 for test.

Monday

1. Show one hundred and ten on the abacus.

2. What number is bigger than 19 by 30? _____

3. 74 is greater than 50 by _____.

4. What time is $1\frac{1}{2}$ hours after 3 o'clock? ☐ : ☐

5. Count the money. _____

6. If I bought one net of pears, how much change would I get from €2? _____

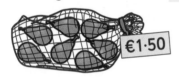

€1·50

7. 12 is half of _____.

8. 50cm _____ $\frac{1}{2}$metre (<, >, =)

9. $\frac{1}{4}$kg of sugar costs 20c. How much for $\frac{1}{2}$kg? _____

10. 56 − 30 = _____

11. Emily had 18c.
She saved 26c more.
She then bought a pen for 21c.
How much has she left? _____

12. There were 26 scarves in a shop.
14 were then sold.
How many are left? _____

/12

Tuesday

1. (28 + 10) − 6 = _____

2.
```
 t u
 3 8
+4 7
```
_____

3. 15 + 15 + _____ → 31 + 4

4. What time is 2 hours after 6 o'clock? ☐ : ☐

5. What is the area of this shape in small squares? _____

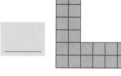

6. _____ is $\frac{1}{4}$ of 16.

7. How much for one banana? _____

€2·00

8. (20 − 8) − 4 = _____

9. 2kg of butter cost €6. How much for 1kg? _____

10. How much more do I need to have €2? _____

The farmer had 12 turkeys and 17 chickens.

11. How many birds does the farmer have altogether? _____

12. If he sold 16, how many birds would he have left? _____

/12

Wednesday

1. (16 + 12) − 10 = _____

2. 41 + 26 + 12 = _____

3. 12 + 12 + _____ = 30

4. What time is $\frac{1}{2}$ an hour after 8 o'clock? [:]

5. 1kg of rice costs €1·90. How much for $\frac{1}{2}$ a kg? _____

6. Show one hundred and six on the abacus.

h t u

7. 39 − 10 = _____

8. Ruth has seventeen 10c coins. How much has she altogether? _____

9. Which has the larger area, (a) or (b)? _____

(a)   (b)

10. $\frac{1}{2}$ of €1·20 = _____

11. There are 8 people at the bus stop. How many eyes in total is that? _____

12. Paul has:

   Robert has:

   How much have they between them? _____

/12

Thursday

1. Show one hundred and twenty-four on the abacus.

h t u

2. What number is bigger than 26 by 20? _____

3. 84 − 42 = _____

4. 12 + 14 + _____ = 40

5. How much for 2 punnets of strawberries? _____

90c

6. 24 is $\frac{1}{2}$ of _____.

7. What is the area of this shape in small squares? _____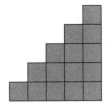

8. $\frac{1}{4}$ of 8 + $\frac{1}{2}$ of 4 = _____

9. How much more do I need to have €2? _____

10. 2kg of meat cost €12. How much for 1kg? _____

There are 11 players on the soccer team.

11. How many football boots do they need in total? _____

12. How many toes does the team have in total? _____

/12

See page 93 for test.

Monday

1. 8 + 6 + _____ = 17

2. What time is it? [:]

3. $\frac{1}{4}$ of 20 + $\frac{1}{2}$ of 8 = _____

4. Draw a line of symmetry.

5. 29 – _____ = 16

6. Is this a right angle?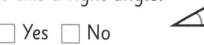

   ☐ Yes ☐ No

7. 18 + _____ = 38

8. How much more do you need to have 1kg of jam? _____

9. Colour the shape that can be used to builds walls.

10. I had €1·50. I spent 75c. I have _____ left.

11. Maria and Jenny had

    between them. How much more do they need to buy the skateboard? _____

12. What is the greatest number of bottles of water you can buy with €2? _____

/12

Tuesday

1. €1·80 + _____ = €2

2. 3 **tens** and 6 **units** = 2 **tens** and _____ **units**

3. 37 – 14 = _____

4. 5, 10, 15, 20, _____, _____

5. How many faces has a cuboid? _____

6. How many cartons make 2 litres? _____

7. Write $\frac{1}{2}$ past 11 in digital time. [:]

8. What is the total height of the teddies? _____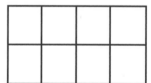

9. Colour $\frac{1}{4}$ of this shape.

10. 29 + 17 = _____

There are 4 children and 2 adults at the kitchen table.

11. Each of them gets a knife and fork. How many knives and forks is that in total? _____

12. If each of them then gets a spoon, how many pieces of cutlery is there in total? _____

/12

Wednesday

1. €1·15 + [____] = €2·00

2. 64 − 20 = [____]

3. (14 + 4) − [____] = 12

4. Is this shape a cylinder or a cone?
[_____]

5. Draw a line of symmetry.

6. How many tins make a litre? [____]

$\frac{1}{4}l$

7. Write $\frac{1}{2}$ past ten in digital time. [:]

8. 20cm + 10cm + [____] = 50cm

9. Colour half of the square.
[ ]

10. 120, 130, [____], 150

11. What is the greatest number of rulers I can buy with €2? [____]

€1·25

12. Daddy hung 2 shirts on the clothes line on Monday, 2 on Tuesday and 2 on Wednesday. How many did he hang on Thursday to have a total of 12 shirts on the line? [____]

/12

Thursday

1. What is the area of this coloured shape in small squares? [____]
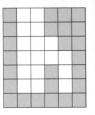

2.
```
t u
 7 3
+2 9
____
```

3. 14c + 14c + [____] = 40c

4. How many numbers on 2 clocks? [____]

5. Draw a line of symmetry.
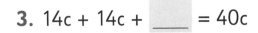

6. 46, 48, [____], 52

7. Write $\frac{1}{2}$ past eight in digital time. [:]

8. How many legs on 4 cows and 2 dogs? [____]

9. $\frac{1}{2} + \frac{1}{2}$ = [____]

10. 90 − 10 → 40 + [____]

2l   1l $\frac{1}{2}l$

11. How many saucepans would it take to fill the bucket? [____]

12. How many teapots can be filled from the bucket? [____]

/12

See page 94 for test.

Monday

1. 70 + ____ = 78

2. 12 + 4 + 11 → 11 + 4 + ____

3. Take 3 from the number of children in your class. ____

4. How many legs on 2 tables and 3 stools? ____

5. (17 + 16) − 15 = ____

6. If you drink $\frac{1}{4}$ l from this bottle, how much would be left? ____

7. If 28 birds were on a wire and 13 flew away, how many would be left? ____

8. How many right angles in a square? ____

9. 16, 20, 24, ____

10. Hannah has eight 20c coins. How much does she have in total? ____

11. There were 38 blue balloons and 36 red balloons hanging from the walls. 40 of them burst. How many balloons are left? ____

12. If Liam starts at the bottom and climbs 9 steps, then climbs 4 more and goes down 10, on what numbered step does he end up? ____

/12

Tuesday

1. What time is 3 hours after 8 o'clock? [:]

2. 31 + 40 = ____

3. $\frac{1}{2}$ of €1·50 = ____

4. How many edges has a cuboid? ____

5. Show 197 on the notation board.

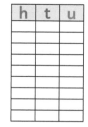

h	t	u

6. Which is greater,
(a) 3 groups of 5 or
(b) 5 groups of 2? ____

7. What is the area of this coloured shape in small squares? ____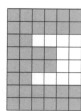

8. 6, 9, 12, ____

9. How much change will I get from €2 if I buy 2 punnets of blueberries? ____

10. 79 − 27 = ____

A train left Dublin for Dundalk at [6:30].

11. The journey takes $1\frac{1}{4}$ hours. At what time is the train due to arrive in Dundalk? [:]

12. If the train is delayed by 1 hour in Drogheda, at what time will the train arrive in Dundalk? [:]

/12

Wednesday

1. What number is bigger than 56 by 30? ____

2. Write these numbers in order, starting with the largest: 89, 91, 98, 99.

____ , ____ , ____ , ____

3. What time is it? [:]

4. How much change would you get from €2 if you bought these 3 items? ____

 17c   23c   12c

5. How many minutes in 2 hours and 16 minutes? ____

6. Draw a line of symmetry.

7. Colour half of the set.

8. How many faces have a cuboid and cube altogether? ____

9. What is the 6th month of the year? ____

10. 36 – 21 = ____

11. Peter had 46 marbles. He lost 28 of them and he won 14. How many had he then? ____

12. Jane is a jockey. She came 1st in 18 races, 2nd in 9 races and 3rd in 8 races. How many races did she take part in? ____

/12

Thursday

1. Show 194 on the abacus.

2. (17 + 2) – 7 = ____

3. How much change would you get from €2 if you bought these 3 pieces of fruit? ____

 19c   21c   7c

4. 76 – 12 = ____

5. 13 + 12 + ____ = 30

6. Round 25 to the nearest 10. ____

7. Colour $\frac{1}{4}$ of the lemons.

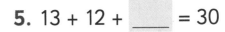

8. 9, 18, 27, ____

9. How many days in 4 weeks? ____

10. This is the month of May. What month will it be 2 months from now? ____

In school one day, there were 56 children on the yard, 21 in the hall and 33 in the library.

11. How many children were in school that day? ____

12. If 15 children had been absent that day, how many children attend the school? ____

/12

See page 95 for test.

Week 1 Test

1. Show 32 on the notation board.

t	u

2. 2 + 6 = _____

3. 3 add 4 = _____

4. It is _____ o'clock.

5. Draw a rectangle.

6. Circle the odd number.

14   13   18   12

7. 14 take away 1 = _____

8. Count the money. _____

9. Colour the fifth cat.

10. Draw the other half of this picture.

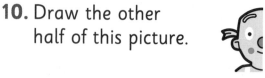

11. Write the missing numbers.

34, 35, _____, _____, 38

12. Tick ☑ the heavier animal.

☐   ☐

Problems

13. Eoghan has six toy cars.
Patrick has four toy cars.
How many cars have they altogether? _____

14. Mammy had eight balloons.
Two of the balloons burst.
How many balloons were left? _____

15. Tamara had twelve stickers.
Mammy gave her four more.
How many had she then? _____

/15

Week 2 Test

1. 7 + 8 = ____

2. Take 9 from 14. ____

3. Colour the rectangle green.

4. What time is it?
____ o'clock

5. 6 + 6 + 6 = ____

6. How many corners has a triangle? ____

7. Which bucket holds more? ____

(a)

(b)

8. Which is the 5th month of the year?
☐ June
☐ May
☐ April

9. Write the numeral thirteen. ____

10. Show 46 on the abacus.

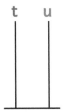

t u

11. Count the money. ____

12. 7, 10, 13, ____, 19

Problems

13. Paul had 5c.
His mammy gave him 10c more.
How much money had he then? ____

14. James got a job cleaning windows.
He cleaned 5 windows on Monday,
8 on Tuesday and 7 on Wednesday.
How many windows did he clean altogether? ____

15. There were 10 apples in a box.
4 of them were bad.
How many good apples were in the box? ____

/15

1. Draw hands on the clock to show $\frac{1}{2}$ past 10.

2. 4 **tens** 8 **units** = _____

3. 7 + 4 = _____

4. 10 – 10 = _____

5. How much for the train and the car altogether? _____

15c   14c

6. Colour the third duck.

7. _____ + _____ = 8 so
   $\frac{1}{2}$ of 8 is _____.

8. Colour the 10c coins to make 40c.

9. Which day comes before Thursday?

☐ Friday

☐ Wednesday

☐ Tuesday

10. 13 count on 10 = _____

11. Colour the longer scarf blue.

12.
```
  t u
  3 2
+ 1 4
_____
```

Problems

13. There were 8 birds on a tree. 4 flew away. How many were left on the tree? _____

14. 12 eggs fit in a tray. I have 6 eggs. How many more eggs do I need to fill the tray? _____

15. There are 5 spots on a ladybird. How many spots on 2 ladybirds? _____

/15

Week 4 Test

1. Add 7 and 9. _____

2. Subtract 7 from 18. _____

3. Draw hands on the clock to show $\frac{1}{2}$ past 12.

4. How many? _____

5. Colour $\frac{1}{2}$ of this set of stars.

6. Which is the 11th month of the year?

☐ October

☐ July

☐ November

7. Colour the coins to make 18c.

8. Name the shape. _____

9. 5 **tens** 2 **units** = _____

10. 50 + 7 = _____

11.
```
 t u
 6 8
+2 1
_____
```

12. Which is heavier? _____

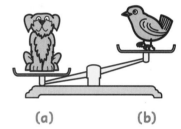

(a)　　　(b)

Problems

13. There were 20 people at a match on Saturday. There were 10 more people at a match on Sunday. How many people were at the match on Sunday? _____

14. Harry decided to count the money in his money box. He had two 10c coins, five 2c coins and one 20c coin. How much money had Harry altogether? _____

15. Jane read 5 pages of her book on Monday, 8 pages on Tuesday and 10 pages on Wednesday. How many pages did she read altogether? _____

/15

1. Count the money. ____

2. 8 + 8 = ____

3. 14 take away 6 = ____

4. 48 = ____ tens ____ units

5. Colour the sphere.

6. Write these numbers in order, starting with the largest:
38, 18, 58, 88, 68.
____ , ____ , ____ , ____ , ____

7. Write the numeral twenty-four. ____

8. Colour $\frac{1}{2}$ the set.

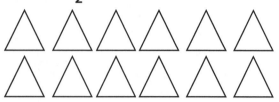

9.
```
 t u
 2 5
+3 2
─────
```
____

10. 15, 20, ____ , 30, ____

11. Fill in the missing sign (<, >, =).

18 ____ 5 + 12

12. Draw hands on the clock to show half an hour earlier than half past 2.

Problems

13. What must I add to 9 to make 19? ____

14. There were 14 flowers in a box.
Mammy picked half of them.
How many did she pick? ____

15. There are 12 red marbles, 13 blue marbles and 14 green marbles in a jar.
How many marbles altogether are in the jar? ____

/15

1. How many 5c coins make up 30c? ____

2. 15, 25, 35, 45, ____

3. 45 + 22 = ____

4. Fill in the missing sign (<, >, =).

7 + 4 ____ 15 − 4

5. Subtract 8 from 33. ____

6. Write these numbers in order, starting with the smallest:
25, 41, 36, 21, 40.

____ , ____ , ____ , ____ , ____

7. Colour $\frac{1}{2}$ of the set.

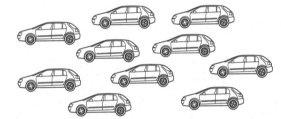

8. What time is it?

____ past ____

9. How many corners has a cube? ____

10. A car weighs:

☐ less than 1kg.

☐ more than 1kg.

☐ about 1kg.

11. Write the number that comes just before 23. ____

12. Count the money. ____

Problems

13. A baker made 23 buns.
If he then sold 9 buns,
how many buns had he left? ____

14. Amanda had 31 stamps.
She lost 10.
How many stamps has she left? ____

15. A farmer had 38 cows.
She sold 16 of them.
How many cows had she then? ____

/15

71

1. 4, 6, 8, _____

2. When I add an odd number and an even number, the answer is always _____ (odd/even).

3. Fill in the missing numbers from this section of the hundred square.

17		19
	28	
		39

4. 73 + 7 = _____

5. 25 − 9 = _____

6. Which day comes after Wednesday?
- ☐ Friday
- ☐ Tuesday
- ☐ Thursday

7. December is in the season of _____.

8. Fill in the missing sign (<, >, =).

9 + 3 _____ 5 + 4

9. A square has _____ corners.

10. Draw hands on the clock to show $\frac{1}{2}$ an hour later than 4 o'clock.

11. Count the money. _____

12.   t u
    6 3
 +2 1
 _____

Problems

13. Anna had 20c. She bought 2 pencils. How much change did she get back? _____

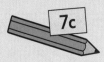
7c

14. A farmer had 18 sheep, 12 cows and 14 goats. How many animals had she altogether? _____

15. There are 36 sweets in jar A and 12 sweets in jar B. How many more sweets are there in jar A than in jar B? _____

/15

1. Draw a line of symmetry.

2. 12 + 9 → 15 + _____

3.

t	u
4	5
+5	2

4. Draw hands on the clock to show $\frac{1}{2}$ past 9.

5. Colour $\frac{1}{2}$ of the set.

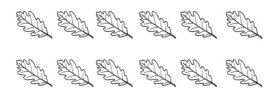

6. How many edges has a cuboid? _____

7. 6 **tens** 9 **units** = _____

8. Show 89 on the abacus.

9. 58 – 38 = _____

10. 45c = ◯ + ◯ + ◯

11. Fill in the missing numbers from this section of the hundred square.

12		14	15
		24	25

12. 66, 67, 68, 69, _____

Problems

pencil

ruler

pencil case

rubber

13. Which two items together cost 31c?

_____ and _____

14. Which two items together cost 15c?

_____ and _____

15. I had €1. I bought all four items. How much change did I get back? _____

/15

1. September is in the season of _____.

2. Draw hands on the clock to show an hour earlier than 7 o'clock.

3. 5 add 9 = ___

4. 15 − ___ = 10

5. Fill in the missing sign (<, >, =).

16 + 2 ___ 18

6. Colour half the teddies red.

7. How many? ___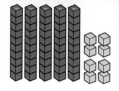

8. 20, 16, 12, ___, ___

9. How many 10c coins make up €1? ___

10. 57 + 22 = ___

11. Which container can hold more water? ___

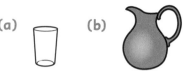

(a)   (b)

12. Colour the cube.

Problems

13. Anne has 24 hair clips. Kate has 12 fewer than Anne. How many hair clips has Kate? ___

14. What is the sum of fifteen and twenty-two? ___

15. A lollipop costs 20c. How many lollipops can I buy with 50c? ___

/15

1. What time is it?

_____

2. How many? _____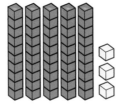

3. 8 add 5 = _____

4. Share 16 strawberries between 2 children. Each child gets _____ strawberries.

5. 17 − 8 = _____

6. 30, 25, 20, _____, _____

7. A bathtub holds:
- ☐ more than 1 litre.
- ☐ less than 1 litre.
- ☐ about 1 litre.

8. How many faces has a cuboid? _____

9. Is M symmetrical?
- ☐ Yes
- ☐ No

10. There are _____ minutes in one hour.

11. Show 79 on the abacus.

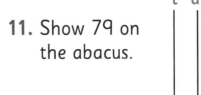

12. Write these numbers in order, starting with the smallest: 44, 49, 36, 41, 32.

_____, _____, _____, _____, _____

Problems

13. James ran for 32 minutes. Conor ran for 25 minutes. How many minutes did they run altogether? _____

14. What is the difference between 21 and 48? _____

15. A football match started at 8 o'clock. It lasted for $1\frac{1}{2}$ hours. At what time did the match finish? _____

/15

Week 11 Test

1. Show 94 on the abacus.

t u

2. Circle the even number.

    45 98 47 31

3. 6 + 7 _____ 14 − 9 (<, >, =)

4. t u
    6 5
   +2 9
   _____

5. Fill in the missing numbers from this section of the hundred square.

47		
57		
		69

6. What day comes just after Wednesday? _____

7. Draw hands on the clock to show $\frac{1}{2}$ past 3.

8. 59 − 4 = _____

9. Which pencil is longer? _____

(a)

(b)

10. Colour $\frac{1}{2}$ the set. _____ is $\frac{1}{2}$ of 16.

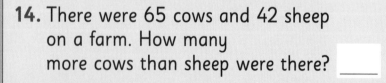

11. 12 + 4 + 7 = _____

12. A house is:

☐ more than 1 metre tall.

☐ less than 1 metre tall.

☐ about 1 metre tall.

Problems

13. A bar of chocolate costs 32c.
Jenny has 20c.
How much more does she need to have enough to buy the chocolate bar? _____

14. There were 65 cows and 42 sheep on a farm. How many more cows than sheep were there? _____

15. Ciara has 18 crayons, John has 15 and Maria has 20. How many crayons have they altogether? _____

/15

Week 12 Test

1. Colour the oval.

2. How many? _____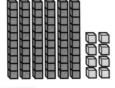

3. 15 take away 5 = _____

4. Fill in the missing numbers from this section of the hundred square.

45	46		
		57	58
65			68

5. Draw hands on the clock to show one hour later than 9 o'clock.

6. 6 + 6 + 6 + 6 = _____

7. What do you see top left?

_____

8. What do you see bottom right? _____

9. A box of cornflakes is the same shape as a _____ .

10. 9 – 3 _____ 10 – 5 (<, >, =)

11.   t u
    5 6
 – 2 4
_____

12. Colour $\frac{1}{2}$ of the set.

_____ is $\frac{1}{2}$ of _____ .

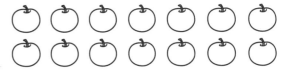

Problems

13. The shopkeeper sold 16 cards on Thursday, 12 on Friday and 18 on Saturday. How many did she sell in total? _____

14. Find the difference between 26 and 53. _____

15. What must I add to 38 to make 65? _____

/15 77

Week 13 Test

1. Count the money. [____]

2. Draw the least number of coins needed to make 80c.

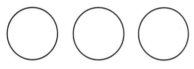

3. What time is it?

[_____]

4. $6 + 4 +$ [____] $= 18$

5. How many? [____] \|\|\|\| \|\|\|\| \|\|\|\| \|\|\|

6. Circle the odd number.

   38   32   35   36

7. Write the number shown on the notation board. [____]

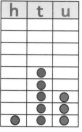

h	t	u

8. Tick the shape of a television screen.

9. How many corners has a cube? [____]

10. t u

    6 6

 +2 4

 [____]

11. 5, 10, 15, [____], 25

12. Draw a line of symmetry.

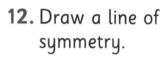

Problems

13. There are 6 apples, 10 oranges and 3 pears in a fruit bowl. How many pieces of fruit are there altogether? [____]

14. Emma goes swimming on Monday, Tuesday and Wednesday. She spends 20 minutes swimming each of these days. How long does she spend swimming altogether each week? [____]

15. Grace had 46 sweets. She gave 21 of them to her friends. How many has she left? [____]

/15

Week 14 Test

1. Draw the least number of coins needed to make 27c.

2. Add 10 to 24. ____

3. Write the number shown on the notation board. ____

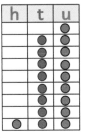

4. 25, 20, 15, ____, ____

5. 8 + 3 + ____ = 15

6. Write the numeral seventy-nine.

____

7. 10 + 3 ____ 20 − 8 (<, >, =)

8. Tick the shapes that are divided in half.

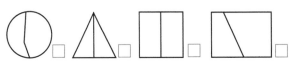

9. How many cubes balance the teddy bear?

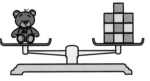

____

10. t u
   6 6
 +2 4

____

11. 4 **tens** 17 **units**

= ____ **tens** ____ **units**

12. Tick the 2-D shape that looks like an orange.

Problems

13. A litre of milk costs 20c. How much for two litres? ____

14. How many legs have two dogs and two cats? ____

15. I had 36 stickers. Mammy gave me 29 more. How many had I then? ____

/15

79

1. Count the money. [____]

2. 10 + 5 → [____] − 5

3. 19 − 2 [____] 7 + 7 (<, >, =)

4. Draw hands on the clock to show $\frac{1}{2}$ an hour earlier than $\frac{1}{2}$ past 11.

5. Draw a line of symmetry.

6. Write these numbers in order, starting with the smallest: 55, 51, 60, 58.

[____] , [____] , [____] , [____]

7. I am a 3-D shape. I can roll, slide and stack. I am a:

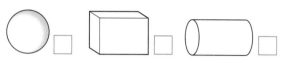

8. 13 + 22 + 33 = [____]

9. 14 + [____] = 20

10. 176 = [____] hundred [____] tens [____] units

11. Write the number shown on the notation board.

[____]

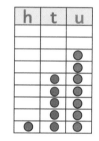

12. October is in the season of [_____].

Problems

13. What is the most popular animal? [_____]

14. What is the least popular animal? [_____]

15. How many children took part in the survey? [____]

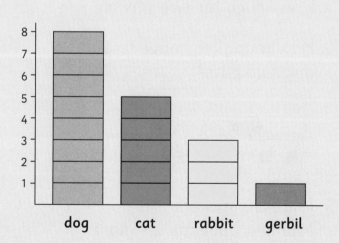

Favourite animal

/15

Week 16 Test

1. 9 + 6 = ____

2. 3, 6, 9, ____ , ____

3. 17 take away 8 = ____

4. 12 − 4 ____ 10 + 2 (<, >, =)

5. Draw hands on the clock to show one hour later than $\frac{1}{2}$ past 11.

6.
```
 t u
 3 7
 2 5
+4 1
_____
```

7. Colour $\frac{1}{4}$ of the circles.

8. What month comes just after June? _____

9. How much change will I get from 50c if I buy one apple? _____

42c

10. Write these numbers in order, starting with the largest: 61, 56, 65, 58, 59.

____ , ____ , ____ , ____ , ____

11. $\frac{1}{2}$ of 12 = ____

12. Is this shape cut in quarters?

☐ Yes
☐ No

Problems

Fun park rides

Rock 'n' Tug	25c
Bumper Boats	50c
Loop the Loop	35c

13. How much does it cost for 2 children to go on the Rock 'n' Tug? ____

14. How much change will I get from 50c if I go on the Loop the Loop? ____

15. I have €1. How many times can I go on the Bumper Boats? ____

/15

1. 9 + 9 + 9 =

2. 12 take away 3 =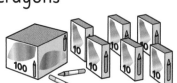

3. What time is it?

4. How many crayons are there?

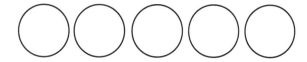

5. Draw a line of symmetry.

M

6. Draw the least number of coins needed to make 97c.

◯ ◯ ◯ ◯ ◯

7. A pineapple weighs:

☐ less than 1kg.

☐ more than 1kg.

☐ about 1kg.

8. 22 + 47 =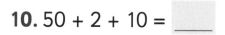

9. Circle the even number.

21   33   28   37

10. 50 + 2 + 10 = _____

11. How long is the pencil? _____ cm

12. 12 – 4 _____ 10 – 3 (<, >, =)

Problems

13. Linda had 17 seashells. Brad had 24 seashells. How many seashells did they have altogether? _____

14. Daniel had some fish in a fish tank. His daddy gave him 12 more. Now he has 26 fish. How many fish had Daniel to begin with? _____

15. Michael's flight was due to take off at 6 o'clock. The flight was delayed by 2 hours. At what time did the flight take off? _____

/15

1. 6 + 8 + 2 = ____

2. 15, 20, 25, ____, ____, 40

3. Draw hands on the clock to show 1 hour earlier than $\frac{1}{2}$ past 4.

4. What 3-D shape do you see? ____

5. Colour the heavier object.

6.
```
  t u
  5 7
 -2 4
 ____
```

7. Today is Wednesday. Tomorrow is _____.

8. Colour $\frac{1}{4}$ of the buttons.

9. Draw the least number of coins needed to make 67c.

○ ○ ○ ○

10. Measure this line. ____ cm

_____

11. $\frac{1}{2}$ of ____ = 10

12. 10 – 3 ____ 12 – 2 (<, >, =)

Problems

13. Harry had €1. He bought a copybook for 75c. How much had he left? ____

14. Colette had 39 marbles. She lost 12 of them. How many marbles does she have left? ____

15. Paul swam 24 lengths of the pool, Tadhg swam 14 lengths and Diarmuid swam 9 lengths. How many lengths did they swim altogether? ____

/15

Week 19 Test

1. t u
      8 9
    −3 4
    _____

2. How many faces has a cuboid? _____

3. My pencil weighs:
    ☐ less than 1kg.
    ☐ more than 1kg.
    ☐ about 1kg.

4. Draw a line of symmetry.

5. Draw hands on the clock to show $\frac{1}{2}$ an hour later than 6 o'clock.

6. $\frac{1}{2}$ of 8 = _____

7. Measure this line. _____ cm

8. €1 + 20c + 5c + 2c = _____

9. Draw the next shape in the pattern.
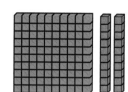 _____

10. 16 + _____ = 23

11. 4, 8, 12, 16, _____

12. How many? _____

Problems

13. There were 23 children playing in the park.
    18 more children came along.
    How many children were there then? _____

14. John had 56 stamps.
    He lost 24 of them.
    How many stamps had he then? _____

15. If 1 litre of milk costs 40c,
    how much would 2 litres cost? _____

84

/15

1. How many corners has a square? _____

2. Circle the digit in the units place: 161.

3. Draw a line of symmetry.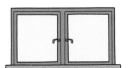

4.
```
 t u
 5 9
-2 7
_____
```

5. 16 + _____ = 25

6. How many edges has a cone? _____

7. 8, 16, 24, _____, 40

8. Draw the least number of coins needed to show 82c.

9. March is in the season of _____.

10. What time is it? _____

11.
```
 t u
 1 8
 2 6
+2 5
_____
```

12. $\frac{1}{4}$ of 20 = _____

Problems

13. John bought 25 stickers on Monday, 18 on Tuesday and 16 on Wednesday. How many stickers did he buy altogether? _____

14. Marcus had 28 sweets. He gave 16 of them to his friend. How many had he left? _____

15. Jack spent half of his money on a new book. If he had €1 at first, how much was the book? _____

/15

1. Draw hands on the clock to show $\frac{1}{4}$ to 7.

2. $6 + 4 + 10 \rightarrow$ _____ $+ 6 + 4$

3. Circle the digit in the units place: 888.

4. Colour half the circle.

5. $7 + 9 +$ _____ $= 21$

6. Joe has:

How much more does he need to have 50c? _____

7.
```
 t u
 7 8
-3 2
_____
```

8. What is the value of the underlined digit: 94<u>9</u>? _____

9. How many days in 2 weeks? _____

10. What fraction of this square is coloured? _____

11. Finish the pattern.

X Y Z X Y _____

12. How many plates do you have in total if you have 26 and 18? _____

Problems

13. There were 16 crows on a wire. 9 flew away. How many are left? _____

14. How much change would you get from 50c if you spent 27c in the shop? _____

15. How much will it cost to buy a pear, an orange and a plum? _____

 20c
 62c
 15c

/15

1. Draw the least number of coins needed to make 63c.

2. What time is it?

____ past ____

3. 10 + 8 + ____ = 25

4. How many pieces of chalk are there?

____

5. Write these numbers in order, starting with the smallest: 56, 68, 55, 60.

____, ____, ____, ____

6. The 2nd month of the year is ____.

7. Draw hands on the clock to show **3:30**.

8. Name this shape.

____

9. 47 − 33 = ____

10. Is this a right angle?

☐ Yes
☐ No

11. Circle the number that does not belong: 22, 28, 32, 25.

12. Colour $\frac{1}{4}$ of the bananas.

Problems

TV5

7:00 Cartoon Time
8:00 Match of the Day
10:00 Film: Floppy Feet

13. How long does Cartoon Time last? ____

14. How long does Match of the Day last? ____

15. Floppy Feet ended after 60 minutes. At what time did it end? ____ : ____

/15

1. $\frac{1}{4}$kg + $\frac{1}{4}$kg + 1kg = ____

2. 79 − 16 = ____

3. How many faces has a cuboid? ____

4. Write the time shown on the clock. ____

5. This angle is:

   ☐ bigger than a right angle.
   ☐ smaller than a right angle.

6. 14 + ____ + 6 = 29

7. Write one hundred and seventy-six as a numeral. ____

8. Colour $\frac{1}{4}$ of the flowers.

9. Measure this line. ____ cm

_____

10. t u
      6 9
    −2 3
    ____

11. 13 + 13 + 1 → 20 + ____

12. I have 50c. How much more do I need to buy the car? ____

60c

Problems

13. John got 50c for every day he helped his daddy. How much did he have after 4 days of helping his daddy? ____

14. Jill had 30c, Ann had 50c and Ruth had 40c.
    How much is that in total? ____

15. Today is Friday the 17th of March.
    What date is Monday? ____

/15

1. What is the weight of one tin? ____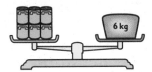

2. 16 + ____ + 2 = 25

3.
```
 t u
 6 4
 1 8
+3 2
____
```

4. How many legs have 4 dogs and 3 birds? ____

5. Write the value of: ____

6. 3 **tens** and 7 **units** =
2 **tens** and ____ **units**

7. What time is it 2 hours later than the time shown on the clock? [:]

8. How many bags of potatoes add up to 10kg? ____

9. How much change will I get from €3 if I spend 65c? ____

10. Colour $\frac{1}{2}$ of the set.

11. Circle the odd number.
66   57   20

12. How many litres in 4 of these bottles? ____ $\frac{1}{2}$ l

Problems

13. A bar of chocolate costs 52c.
Claire has 19c.
How much more does she need to have enough to buy the bar of chocolate? ____

14. What is the difference between 79 and 24? ____

15. There were 47 apples on a tree.
19 fell off.
How many apples are still on the tree? ____

/15

Week 25 Test

1. Fill in the missing numbers from this section of the hundred square.

71		73	
	82		84

2. Write the time half past 2 in digital form. [:]

3. A programme started at $\frac{1}{4}$ to 4 and lasted until $\frac{1}{4}$ past 4. How many minutes did the programme last? ____

4.
```
  t u
  5 4
 -2 8
 ____
```

5. 9, 13, 17, 21, ____

6. If a litre costs €1, how much would $\frac{1}{2}$ a litre cost? ____

7. 10 is $\frac{1}{4}$ of ____.

8. Finish the pattern.

Z Y X Z Y ____

9. 9 **tens** and 2 **units** = 8 **tens** and ____ **units**

10. How many wheels are on one car and two tricycles? ____

11. Show 195 on the notation board.

h	t	u

12. What number is bigger than 55 by 10? ____

Problems

13. There were 16 pegs on a clothes line. Jane put up 7 more. How many pegs are on the line now? ____

14. There were 19 strawberries in a bowl. If I take 15 away, how many are left? ____

15. David had 35 shells. He lost 19. How many shells has he left? ____

/15

Week 26 Test

1. Show 198 on the abacus.

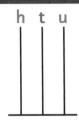

2. How many litres are there? _____

3. How long from $\frac{1}{4}$ past 4 to $\frac{1}{4}$ past 6? _____

4. How much for 2 pens and 3 pencils? _____

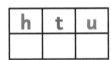 22c 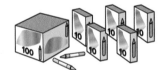 15c

5. How many days in 4 weeks? _____

6. Write the correct number.

h	t	u

7. Divide this rectangle into quarters.

8. 14, 18, 22, _____

9. 13 + 13 + _____ = 30

10.

```
 t u
 9 7
-3 8
____
```

11. Colour $\frac{1}{2}$ the leaf.

12. Today is Friday. What day will it be in two days' time? _____

Problems

13. You need 4 eggs to make a cake. How many eggs do you need to make 2 cakes? _____

14. If a pineapple costs 30c, how much for 3 pineapples? _____

15. If a cow drinks 3 litres of water in a day, how much will the cow drink in a week? _____

/15

91

Week 27 Test

1. 6 **tens** and 4 **units** =
5 **tens** and ____ **units**

2. Write the value of:

____

3. 40 + 15 + 10 = ____

4. What is the area
of the coloured shape
in small squares?

____

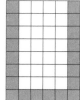

5. Draw a line of
symmetry.

6. Measure this line. ____ cm

_____

7. 7 + 19 + ____ = 30

Number of trees in the park

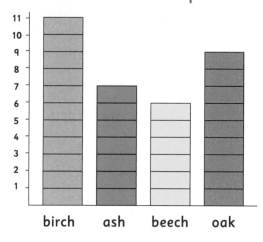

8. Which tree is the
most common? _____

9. Which tree is the
least common? _____

10. How many trees in total
are there in the park? ____

11. Write $\frac{1}{2}$ past eleven in
digital time. [:]

12. 3, 6, 9, 12, ____

Problems

13. Shane wrote down the number 57.
Jan wrote down 71.
How much bigger was Jan's number
than Shane's? ____

14. Jessica spent half of her €1·20 on food.
How much did she spend on food? ____

15. A horse drank 5 litres of water
a day for 3 days.
How many litres is that? ____

/15

Week 28 Test

1. Show one hundred and seventy-one on the abacus.

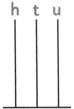

8. t u

$$\begin{array}{r} 9\,6 \\ -1\,9 \\ \hline \end{array}$$

2. What number is bigger than 19 by 30? _____

9. What is the area of the coloured shape in small squares? _____

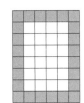

3. 10 + 15 + _____ = 35

10. (25 − 10) + 4 = _____

4. How much for 2 bags of grapes? _____

90c

11. Circle the number in the tens place: 136.

5. 1kg = _____ + $\frac{1}{4}$kg + $\frac{1}{4}$kg

12. How long is the matchstick? _____

6. What time is $1\frac{1}{2}$ hours after 3 o'clock? [:]

7. Draw a cuboid.

Problems

13. By how much is 99 greater than 77? _____

14. Daddy made 12 cupcakes on Saturday and 18 on Sunday. How many cupcakes did he make altogether? _____

15. Aoife has: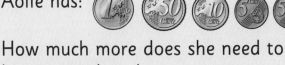

How much more does she need to have enough to buy the smoothie? _____

€2
Smoothie

/15

1. Fill in the missing numbers on this section of the hundred square.

	63		65
72		74	

2.
```
  t u
  8 6
 −1 8
 ____
```

3. 4 + 6 ____ 15 − 5 (<, >, =)

4. If the 12th of June is on a Friday, on what day is the 14th of June? _____

5. Draw a line of symmetry.

6. What time is it? _____

7. 33, 35, 37, ____

8. How many wheels on 6 tricycles? ____

9. 24 − ____ = 12

10. What is the total height of the dolls? ____

20cm 25cm

11. Write the missing month.

January, February, March, _____, May

12. This angle is:

☐ bigger than a right angle.
☐ smaller than a right angle.

Problems

13. Pete had 23c.
He got 10c from his mammy.
He then spent 12c.
How much has he left? ____

14. David had 14 copies.
Elaine had 12.
They gave 9 to their teacher.
How many had they left? ____

15. A restaurant sold 9 bottles of orange juice, 4 bottles of water and 5 bottles of apple juice.
How many bottles in total is that? ____

/15

1. (12 + 5) – 13 = ____

2. How much change would you get from €2 if you bought these 3 items? ____

3. 17 + 13 + ____ → 20 + 20

4. How many minutes in 2 hours and 7 minutes? ____

5. Colour the cone.

6. Jill turned 7 on September the 18th. Ellen was 7 exactly three months later. What date is Ellen's birthday? ____

7. Tick the container that holds more.

 ☐ ☐

8. 9, 18, 27, ____

9. Divide the circle in quarters.

10. $\frac{1}{2}$ kg ____ $\frac{1}{4}$ kg (<, >, =)

11. Show 181 on the abacus.

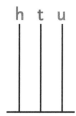

12. What time is it? ____

Problems

13. A television programme started at **8:30** and finished $1\frac{1}{2}$ hours later. At what time did it finish? ☐ : ☐

14. Peter, Paul and Mary had 63c, 22c and 79c between them. How much more do they need to have €2? ____

15. The shopkeeper sold 32 newspapers on Friday and 15 on Saturday. How many newspapers did he sell altogether? ____

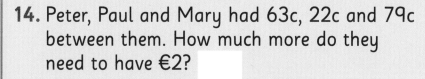

/15